A REBEL *from* RICHES

THE AUTOBIOGRAPHY
of
AN UNPREMEDITATED MONK

By Father Bede Reynolds, O.S.B.
(ne: Kenyon L. Reynolds)

PATRICIA PFITZER REYNOLDS

TO MY WIFE

without whom this story

would not have come about

BECAUSE

she brought me a treasure

more precious than riches.

Peace to you
Father Bede Reynolds OSB

IMPRIMATUR:

Most Rev. James F. Carney, D.D.,
Archbishop of Vancouver.

April 24, 1970.

NIHIL OBSTAT

Daniel J. Carey, D.P.
Censor Librorum
March 21st, L970

IMPRIMI POTEST:

+ Eugéne Medved,O.S.B.
Abbot of Westminster

Contents

Chapter 1

SOME CALL IT LUCK

Late in August, 1945, I went in to lunch at the California Club in Los Angeles. As I sat down at the "Long Table", Dick Griffith of Graves Banning sat down beside me.

"You've certainly given your friends in the investment business plenty to talk about," he said with a chuckle.

As I looked up with interest, he continued: "Here's the gist of the comment: 'Poor old Ken, he's gone completely off the rocker. Here he sits with more money than he will ever spend; free to go where he pleases; do what he pleases; buy what he pleases; and what does he do? He gives his beautiful home in Pasadena to the Archbishop; he gives his summer home on the McKenzie River in Oregon to the Capuchins; he hires an administrator for all his investments; and now he's off to enter a monastery and be a monk. It's understandable that he's pretty hard hit since Patty died, but when a guy has had all the luck he's had, you wouldn't think he'd be *that* far gone'."

Then, Dick leaned close to me and said, "Ken, don't you think it's a little too soon to make such a prodigious decision?"

I answered, "Dick, you know me well enough to know the anwer to that one. They call it 'luck' but my life has been a most amazing sequence of tiny beginnings that have led me, kicking and bucking, into a final situation that is so far removed from anything that I could have planned for myself that I have at last learned to believe that it is really naive to call it luck. The final pattern is too perfect and the beginnings were too innocent and too cute to let me admit that it all comes about by chance. It has taught me that everything that happens to everybody is very much under the control of the One who is the Source of it all. And above all, even when it hurts, it is evidence of a love that puts it beyond the possibility of just happening to happen. You can put yourself in God's hands and profit by it, or you can go it alone and God won't stop you.

"Furthermore, my story has been so improbable and the final result has been so unpredictable and so much more precious than luck, that I think I ought to tell it to the world. It will embarrass God a little at times because He has had to make His part so obvious. But it will be worth it because it will help to bring peace to souls."

Recalling this bit of conversation, it is now high time to tell my story to the world.

My Mother, Frances Arburthnot Llewellyn, was born at Louisville, Kentucky, in 1850. One day, shortly after the close of the Civil War, she was with a group of young ladies who were specifying the qualities of the men they hoped to marry. Finally, one of them turned to Miss Llewellyn and said, "Fanny, you haven't said a word. What kind of a man do you plan to marry?"

"Well," said Fanny, "I haven't thought much about it, but I know three things he's *not* going to be. He's not going to be a Northerner, and he's not going to be a farmer, and he's not going to be younger than I am."

Suppose you had a friend, Henry Graham Reynolds, born in Buffalo, New York, a year younger than Fanny and farming for apples in Michigan, what would you say were the chances of being the seventh child of Henry Reynolds and Fanny Llewellyn? Yes — you have guessed it! I was even "lucky" to be born!

But the odds against it made very little difference to God. He simply arranged it so that Henry Reynolds had enough other things in his favor to overcome Fanny Llewellyn's threefold veto of youngish Yankee farmers. And so they were married at the home of the bride's mother, Mexico, Missouri, on Thursday, September 24th, 1874.

After a ten-month honeymoon in Europe, they spent the next eight years on the farm at Old Mission, Michigan. But while Mother dearly loved her farmer-husband, she never did learn to be quite so fond of farm life. So, it was much to her satisfaction when, in 1885, Father was appointed to the Michigan State

Board of Agriculture. As a result, the family moved to East Lansing where they were installed in "Faculty Row" on the campus of Michigan Agricultural College, as Michigan State University was then called.

The family now boasted three sons, Llewellyn, Robert and Duncan, and two daughters, Jessie, and Margaret. Then God must have said with a chuckle: "I will add two more sons to this dear family who will do things to their religious history that nobody would believe were I to reveal it to them now!"

And so it came about that Graham was born in 1887 and, last and least Kenyon Llewellyn arrived on the scene on the cold and wintry 26th of January, 1892.

Not long after my birth, Father, then only forty-two, began to show symptoms of Parkinson's disease. Then, acting on the advice of his doctor, he resigned his position and took his wife and mother and the five younger children to Southern California to make a new home.

There was, in another part of this California to which the family came, a little girl named Hazel Alice Patricia Pfitzer. She will not enter this story until many other things are told, but when you and I look back over the thread that it weaves, we will be amazed to see how it had to come about because, in God's plan, Patricia was to help to give me a treasure more precious than riches.

After spending the first winter in a rented house in the hubbub of madly growing Los Angeles, Father, seeking a safer moral atmosphere for his family, purchased a twelve-acre orange grove in the nearby quiet town of Pasadena. There, he built a large rambling home to which the family moved in October, 1894.

On this occasion Father noted in his Guest-Book: "The members of the family at that time united in thanksgiving for the blessing of a settled home and in the prayer that the new home, by whomsoever occupied, might always be a scene of loving Christian family unity."

This entry was by no means an empty rhetorical gesture. From the very beginning, family prayer was a daily occurrence

Hello Everybody! Why worry when you are going to be bald anyway?
Ken Reynolds, age 3 months

in the library after breakfast. And this was not the only spiritual example and nourishment furnished by my parents. They were faithful Low-Church Episcopalians and saw to it that their children never failed to attend Sunday School and Church. I attended Church every Sunday when I was young enough to be terrified by the Senior Warden who sat across the aisle from us and whose beard was much more formidable than my father's.

Father was a Christian because he loved Christ. He carried it into his daily life in a way that inspired the same sentiments of sincerity in all of his children.

So this was the home which furnished the background of my earliest memories and the only ones of my darling Mother.

One of the earliest memories in which she figures was my first day at Kindergarten. Mother's presence there is seen through large tears which I was unable to keep back as she stood in the doorway ready to depart and leave me with all these strange children.

There were about twenty children who attended and it was coeducational as was every other school I attended until, at age fifty-six I began to study theology.

I am told that "going-steady" is one of the ill results of coeducation in our day. So perhaps it is incautious for me to disclose my early approval of this so called evil. The fact remains, however, that from then on, I began to deny that all girls looked alike to me. And I have held the same conviction ever since. I proved it a few weeks after entering Kindergarten by making, with the help of my grandmother, a lovely little silk doll's quilt for Janie Stimpson.

But that first day, as Mother was leaving, all I can remember was homesick fright.

There are other vivid memories of my Mother of quite a different character. Several of them involve scars on my person which persist until the present day.

One of them in which God's hand is obvious came about on a Saturday afternoon a couple of weeks after my sixth birthday. I was very proud of my success at riding my sister Margaret's bicycle even though I had to stand on the pedals because I could not reach the seat. I dashed into the house and called Mother and Father out to the curb to watch me prove my prowess.

While they were standing there ready to cheer, I mounted the bike and rode down the driveway into the street and WHAM! into a loaded "Express" wagon exactly between the horse and the front wheels. Imagine Mother and Father standing there to watch the narrow steel tires of both front and rear wheels pass over my head and chest! Father dashed out and picked me up thinking that I was dead.

I must have fainted from fright before the crash came and remained unconscious until mid-morning of the following day when I was surprised to have Mother kiss me and shush me back into bed when I started to get up. In further proof that all this happened to me, there is a scar over my left eye and a wheel-track on my chest that makes every examining physician raise his eyebrow for an explanation. I also have a newspaper clipping from the Los Angeles Sunday Times with a headline calling six-year-old Kenyon Reynolds "A MIGHTY LUCKY BOY".

The next incident I should be ashamed to relate about any other member of the family than myself because it displays a little numskull! But perhaps it is in keeping with my present wish to cultivate the virtue of humility to tell the story about myself.

It pertains to a long-handled pruning hook which had a shaft about eight feet long and was standing against a lean-to at the side of the barn with the knife reaching a couple of feet above the roof and the operating lever inaccessible to me behind a small pile of lumber. Wishing to do some fancy pruning of my own, I climbed to the roof of the shed and, firmly grasping the hook with the index finger of my right hand and the shaft with my left hand, I gave a mighty heave almost immediately accompanied by a mighty roar of something else beside joy!

There is, in Catholic clerical parlance, a half-jocular expression which designates the left eye as the "canonical eye" and the index finger as the "canonical finger". The reason for this terminology is that these members are essential for the proper celebration of the Sacrifice of Mass. The scar which gives evidence of my encounter with the pruning hook extends three-quarters of the way around my right index finger. That, together with the wheel-track over my left eye, does remind me occasionally of the infinite goodness of God.

All of these incidents are fragmentary but I tell them because of their importance for my whole life of these brief years of my Mother's influence.

One little episode stands out in exact detail. I can see her now as she stood there at the foot of my bed. A lovely gentle expression of tenderness vying with an anxious urge to be firm suffused her beautiful face, youthful yet mature and motherly.

My brother Graham, poor lad, was burdened with a little brother who was mortally fearful of the dark. My frenzy at being left alone in the dark brought it about that ten-year-old Graham was saddled with the onus of going to bed with his little brother of six. It certainly is not surprising that there were times when his impatience caused him to pester this blight to his freedom in a way that brought forth yowls of disapproval from said "blight".

It was one of these encounters which had brought Mother to our room on this occasion. But the thing that has anchored it forever in my memory was that she said so solemnly: "What are you two boys going to do when I am gone?" At that time she was forty-eight. How little did any one of us imagine that in a few short months she would be "gone", as I firmly believe, to heaven. And still less could *she imagine* what these two boys *would* do; namely, return to the Faith lost by her Welsh forbears and end, both of them, by becoming Catholic priests.

How strange it is that my memory has immortalized all these trivial things connected with her who gave me so much of my start in life. And yet, of her death on Sunday, January 8th, 1899, I have no direct memory whatsoever. It came about as the sequel to a horse runaway when she and Father were out for a Sunday drive three weeks earlier. Both were severely injured but Father was able to be up and around by Christmas. Mother seemed to recover quite slowly, but by the third Sunday she was sitting up and Father felt that it was safe to leave her so that he could go to Church. Soon after he left, however, Mother's heart seemed to give her great pain and Graham was sent on the run to summon Father. She was unconscious when they returned and died a few minutes later.

On the marker of her grave Father had inscribed the verse from the Book of Proverbs describing the "Valiant Woman" — "Her children shall rise and call her blessed: her husband also, and he praises her." No epitaph could be more appropriate for the first woman I loved.

And so it was that a new phase of my life began as my Father took over with his eldest daughter not yet sixteen and his youngest son not yet seven.

My first vivid memory of this half-orphan "Life With Father" pictures him coming in haste to my bedside a few weeks after Mother's death. There, he found me in utter panic fighting madly to get more air into my lungs through a wind-pipe almost closed by an attack of "croup". Father, with almost Mother's gentleness, took me in his arms and squeezed great globs of vaseline into my mouth. Gradually the choking subsided and I returned to almost normal breathing. Then, after a week in bed, I was "as good as new". Father and I both long remembered that experience and it added to our cherished memories of my Mother who had always been a tower of strength in such emergencies.

The Boy Scouts of America came into being on February 8th, 1910, two weeks after my eighteenth birthday. So, official Scouting never came my way. But in Father, God provided me with far better childhood training than would be possible in any organizational program. Father and I became a two-man Scout Group; he the Master, I the pre-cub, cub, candidate, tenderfoot, and on up to Eagle and Explorer.

In all this my Father's example of patience, forbearance, and charity, coupled with good firm discipline, has stood me in good stead many a time as an employee, a husband, a business executive, and finally, as a monk!

Father took me to Follows Camp on the San Gabriel River when I was nine years old. I can still remember how my heart almost jumped out of my chest when I hooked my first rainbow trout on a fly. I have never ceased to regard fly-fishing as the most perfect sport which God has provided for His children to enjoy.

A brand-new phase of my life began at midyear, 1903. Father, remembering the benefits he had gained by a year of study at Wiesbaden, Germany, in his youth, decided to take Margaret and Jessie for a two year sojourn abroad. Thus it came about that I went to live with my brother Duncan and his wife, Estelle at their new home in Pasadena.

Estelle had been a housewife for two years, but this was her very first experience at taking charge of an eleven-year-old. The situation was aggravated by the fact that this eleven-year-old had been without a mother for almost five years. The going was a bit rough for both of us but Estelle soon learned that financial inducement gave better control over me than any other kind of restraint. She was a stern disciplinarian in that she never relaxed one iota from the system of fines under which my weekly allowance was encumbered.

Holding a fork in the wrong position or the wrong hand cost a penny each time. Taking food before unfolding my napkin cost another penny. If I was not in the bath-tub by four o'clock on Saturday afternoon, a nickle was lost from my forty-five-cents-per-week allowance. In that case, however, Estelle would give a hint of impending danger about three o'clock.

Attendance at Church was not on Estelle's penal code, but that seems the one thing I did not have to be urged to do. I knew it to be my Father's wish, and my own conscience was beginning to reach out for spiritual support. Father had given me a Bible just before his departure and I began at Genesis, Chapter one, verse one, and read a chapter every night before going to bed.

The major event of that year was the birth of my first niece. I was quite as proud of her as were her parents and tried to spoil her much more vigorously than they did. She was probably the most photographed baby in Southern California prior to Shirley Temple.

As a result of the arrival of little Betty and Estelle's indisposition shortly thereafter, we all moved to the old Wallace Ranch, home of Estelle's parents in Alhambra. That year of my life spent on an old California orange ranch was filled with new experiences remembered with great delight.

Outstanding among these experiences was my first ride in an automobile. Walter Wallace, Estelle's younger brother, had somehow acquired possession of a steam-driven "Mobile Surrey". It had neither top nor windshield; they were "extras" in 1904. This was not a new machine and it required quite elaborate preparations for each run.

Most of the rides were after supper, so the acetylene side-lamps had to be cleaned and charged with carbide and water. One or more of the tires nearly always needed attention with a hand pump. The boiler water and fuel pump had to be checked Then, when all was in readiness, the fuel generating tube was placed in a pan on the ground and gasoline and a match applied to bring the tube up to heat. It was then inserted in the burner and the fire was ignited in the boiler which was under the front seat beside the engine.

When steam was up to pressure there were usually six passengers on hand and the pleasure ride would begin. That little two cylinder double-acting steam engine had a sweeter sound than any other motor I have ever known; and the twenty miles per hour which it produced was plenty for the dirt roads, open front, and dim lights which went with those rides.

Father and Jessie and Margaret returned from Europe in the spring of 1905. It was then that Father proposed to take Graham and me on a two-months tour of the United States. My delight at the prospect of such a trip was blighted by the fact that I had contracted a fanatical fear of thunder and lightning. I had aggravated that fear by reading everything I could get my hands on regarding its vagaries.

Our departure was scheduled for mid-June and I knew from my reading that thunderstorms would be rampant all over the East. I tried desperately to think up some reason for postponing the date of departure, but I was equally ashamed to admit the real reason.

At length, my boyish desire for the trip prevailed. It was to be my first look outside Los Angeles County since babyhood. But that inner dread was hard to fight down as we pulled out of Pasadena on the Santa Fe "Overland". We did, indeed, have plenty of thunderstorms. My terror was perhaps calloused but far from cured. But the joys of that trip far outweighed the fears.

Upon our return, Father once more began to plan a new home. Finally a lot was purchased on West California Street and building was begun early in 1906.

During the building interim we lived in a rented house quite near St. Andrew's Catholic Church. One Sunday afternoon Father and Graham and I were passing when people were pouring into the Church so we followed them in. It was the first time I had even been inside a Catholic Church. In fact, we had regarded Catholics as a sort of semi-dangerous immigrants.

This particular ceremony ended with Benediction. I had never heard of the Presence of God in the consecrated Host, so I had no idea what was going on when the monstrance was raised in Benediction over the adoring congregation. But I still have a mind picture that features that particular elevated Host. I was also impressed by the devotion of the worshippers. They did not look even remotely dangerous to me.

We moved into our new home in November, 1906. Father's first project was the construction of a tournament-sized cement tennis court. This helped to make the remainder of my high school days very eventful and filled to the brim with interest. There was much tennis, many parties and dances, house-parties at Catalina Island and much else that would be utterly boring to recount in detail.

By the time my graduation day arrived I had made up my mind that I wanted to be an engineer. I hoped to be admitted at Cornell University where by brother Robert had graduated in electrical engineering some ten years before.

I was only seventeen when I graduated from high school and Father thought it would be wise for me to wait one year before entering college. This appealed to me so Father wrote to Llewellyn who was then a mining engineer in charge of a gold and silver mine at Mogollon, New Mexico. Llew replied that he could give me a job as timberman's helper for four dollars per day. That was about twice what I could have earned in a local job. It would also give me a good opportunity to find out how I liked the mining profession. So, on August 25th, 1909, I stepped out from under my Father's protecting arm and began to find out what it would be like to grow up.

And that gives the setting for the rest of my story. I hope that you will come along with me and see that my "luck" has included some sickness, some sadness, some bereavement, but mostly, all that makes for happiness as the world sees it.

Yes, some call it luck, but I prefer to take the hint of the Gaelic blessing that says: "May the wind be always at your back", and offer my gratitude to the Mighty Wind of Pentecost Who is always at the back of this "Mighty Lucky Boy."

Chapter 2

A YEAR FOR EXPERIENCE

God let me have a gentle introduction to life-in-the-world by giving me my first job, as it were, on a platter. My brother Llewellyn was Mine Superintendent at the Fanny Champion Mine at Mogollon, New Mexico. He had assured me of a job so I knew that all I had to do was to present myself at his doorstep at my own convenience and he would do the rest. It was not until I began to look for my second job that I realized what a tremendous advantage this was.

Access to Mogollon in 1909 was by train from Deming, New Mexico, to Silver City, thence by stagecoach over ninety miles of desert and mountain road. By changing horses six times, the trip was made in fifteen hours.

So, there was high adventure for me in spending all day and part of the night traveling through country laden with legend of western frontier life. It ended in a canyon which had been a stronghold of the hostile Apache Indians under Geronimo who terrorized the inhabitants of Arizona and New Mexico at the close of the last century.

I stepped down from the stagecoach at Mogollon about ten o'clock in the evening of the last day of August, 1909, and was greeted by Llewellyn. We started off into the dark on foot up a very steep road that led to the Fanny Champion Mine. I very soon found myself quite out of breath and Llew had to recall that his little brother was not yet acquainted with an altitude of over seven thousand feet.

As we climbed another three or four hundred feet in altitude, the increasing roar of the stamp-mill told us that we were nearing our destination. Soon the lights of the mill draped themselves down the hillside in front of us and I was introduced to its perpetual atmosphere of noise.

Fanny Champion mine and mill at Mogollon, New Mexico.

Next day, after a brief tour with Llew around the working stopes at the two-hundred-foot level, I was assigned to help a crew of timbermen who were working there. This crew was shoring up the ceiling beside a ventilating shaft. By the light of our candles, this shaft looked like a black square of nothingness. I was told that its bottom was five hundred feet below. The edge of that black opening had the same effect on my insides that its depth would have caused if I could have seen its bottom. By the time we came to the surface at the lunch hour, I was quite certain that I did *not* want to be a mining engineer!

The "shooting" of the morning's work was all done during the noon-hour. That means that the holes drilled in the ore-body during the morning had been charged with dynamite and they are fired as soon as all of the men are checked out at the top of the mine shaft. Air compressors are kept running to drive out the nitro-glycerine fumes, but they are only partially effective. Within a half hour after going underground after lunch, I was so sick that I was useless for the work so the foreman sent me back to the surface. I was thoroughly convinced that four dollars per day was no inducement to work as a timberman's helper.

A fortunate circumstance, such as God was always providing, saved the day for me and helped poor Llew to solve the problem of what to do with his green little brother. The company had just hired a full time assayer, H. N. Reed, who had just arrived and who needed a helper. So, the next day I went to work in the assay office at two dollars per ten-hour day. I was happy that I was never called upon to go underground again!

Work in the assay office was very interesting and instructive. It was really a very busy and well-equipped chemistry laboratory. It had three functions of first importance: first, to determine the gold and silver content of the output of the mine; second, to compare this with the recovery of these metals in the cyanide mill; third, to protect the company from law-suits on account of cyanide poisoning of cattle in the valley of the Rio San Francisco below.

The values in the samples brought to us each day varied from two thousand dollars per ton in the mill concentrates, down to twenty cents per ton in the tailings. So it can be seen that meticulous care was needed to avoid any contamination of one with the other or any mixing of labels or losing of labels. The slightest failure in this regard would not merely render our results worthless; it would make the assay office an enemy instead of an ally.

The assayer and his helper had to observe quite as much

care as do the "clean" nurse and the "dirty" nurse in an operating room.

The experience gained in those few months in that assay office in that far corner of New Mexico taught me a lesson which has profoundly affected my entire life. It has supplemented my motto that success demands the will-to-do-what-it-takes and adds the caution that nothing can be done successfully that is done carelessly. And that is just as true whether I am making love to my wife, deciding to spend a million dollars to build a gasoline plant, or singing a Solemn High Mass. I am grateful to the Wind-At-My-Back for the fumes that made me sick that first half-day in the mine.

This job was also ideal to accomplish the results that Father had wished when suggesting a year of experience between high school and college.

My health was safely assured by plenty of exercise. I sawed wood for the assay furnace and "bucked" thirty or more samples per day through sieves, some as fine as two hundred wires per inch.

Then, as Henry Reed and I became better acquainted and he began to trust his seventeen-year-old helper more and more, he let me do all the various parts of the job until, finally, I was helping to weigh little specks of gold almost too small to see, on scales operated inside a glass case and standing on massive concrete foundations.

All these interesting experiences increased my desire to go to college but I was not attracted to mining engineering. My one day in the mine cured me of that. So, I was not sorry when Llew told me on December 20th that the whole works was to be shut down and my first job had come to an end.

After paying my board bill, I had earned about one hundred dollars which only slightly exceeded the cost of my transportation back to Pasadena, but I came away with a good pocket-full of experience.

My homecoming on Christmas Eve was made joyful by many parties but Father and I were mindful of the fact that another

Henry Reed watching his seventeen year old helper.

nine months would elapse before I would be departing for college and this was not a time for parties but for growing up.

Engineering experience was, of course, my objective but how does one go about it when starting from zero? Once more Providence provided the answer.

The old Los Angeles Aqueduct from Owens Valley was then under construction. They were short of men qualified for surveying parties and were offering assignments as civil service chainman to high school graduates without examination. When I applied at the aqueduct office in Los Angeles, I was taken on as a temporary chainman at seventy dollars per month. My instructions were to report immediately to Mr. Bailey, Field Director of the Locating Division, with headquarters at Lone Pine, California. So it came about that I stepped off the Southern Pacific train at Mojave, California, about midnight of January 12th, 1910, feeling and being exceedingly ill at ease.

This railroad and mining town in the center of the Mojave Desert had waked up to find itself a central distributing point for the entire Los Angeles Aqueduct. Its chief "business" at midnight, however, was to provide eating, drinking and gambling facilities for those "coming" and those "going" as distinguished from those working on the aqueduct.

Here I was, in a business suit and carrying two suitcases. Everyone else was in khaki or jeans and carried a bed roll, large or small, wrapped in canvas. The scene was much more realistic than any Western movie I had ever seen. The drunks and evil looking characters needed no make-up to look fierce to me. If I had known how fierce they really were, I probably would have been paralyzed with fright. This was one of the most evil spots in the West at that time and the morgue was by no means an idle bit of scenery.

I had six hours to wait for the departure of the train on the partially completed branch line to the Owens Valley. My one thought was to put a locked door between myself and all this tumult. I spotted a building labeled DESERT HOUSE — ROOMS, and lost no time to make for the open door. There, after one look inside the bed, I sat till morning writing letters which I fear did not conceal my mournful state of mind. I also said some prayers and resolved that I would see it through. It was a good thing that I was alone. If two of us had been as scared as I was, we would have convinced each other that it was rank folly to go on to Lone Pine.

The branch line train consisted of about sixty freight cars plus one passenger coach hooked between the last freight car and the caboose. When it was finally backed in to the station, every seat was immediately filled and, as nearly as I could determine, I was the only one aboard who had not had at least a morning bracer. It was quite terrifying to me.

At each siding cars were shunted and switched while we sat and shivered and the drinking progressed. The eighty-four miles to the terminus at Little Lake had consumed more than twelve hours when we pulled in to the box-car station well after midwinter darkness had taken over.

I was much relieved to find that the stage driver was sober, but being late, he was in a mad hurry to be on the road and away. He placed me and my two suitcases in the tonneau and we started off at a pace faster than I had ever traveled in an automobile before.

The road between Little Lake and Lone Pine was a topographic phenomenon that no modern mind could even imagine. My experience in the back seat resembled in one respect that of a space-man in orbit. I and my suitcases spent a considerable portion of the time in mid-air, as it were, floating between the top and the floor boards. The effect, however, was quite different. All the properties of gravity remained in force!

We reached Lone Pine without any major accident about 9:00 p.m. After carefully examining myself, I found that I was still able to walk and carry my suitcases across the quarter-mile trail between the town and the headquarters of the Locating Engineer. There, in the office in Mr. Bailey's cottage, I found Mr. Bailey and his two party chiefs, Mr. Baldwin and Mr. Hamilton, poring over a large contour map.

All three looked up as I introduced myself as the new provisional chainman assigned to the party. Looking back on that scene after almost sixty years of experience with all kinds of men, my respect for those three gentlemen is tremendously deepened. I have often wondered, had our positions been reversed, if I would have refrained from uproarious laughter. I doubt very much if any of them had even seen anything that looked less like a qualified civil service chainman. Everything bespoke an experience rating of absolute zero!

In my five months on this job I don't remember seeing anyone else with a suitcase, let alone two! And my city clothes were just as appropriate as "tails and white tie" would have been. Probably my hopeful smile was all that saved the situation from disaster for me. Not one of them showed the surprise and mirth he must have felt. Perhaps their disappointment partially saved the day.

I believe, however, that that first impression must have brought it about that those two party chiefs, both of whom I served under during the next five months, taught me more than did any future boss about how to live with other human beings. I learned a lot about surveying, but I learned a lot more about men! I doubt if I have ever seen anyone who was quite as green as I was then. But the ripening process was immediate and intensive.

Mr. Bailey began it by quietly surmising that I did not have my bed with me so I could sleep in his "guest-room" that night. The guest-room turned out to be a cot in the office and a bucket and basin on the front porch. That brief invitation taught me that the construction personnel on a wilderness project at the beginning of the twentieth century all automatically acquired the status of transient, then euphemistically labeled "bindlestiff". A bed-roll was as much a part of the equipment of an engineer as it was for a cook-house flunky.

I did have fairly suitable work clothes acquired at Mogollon. This helped for my first appearance in the cook-tent next morning and did not prejudice my team mates, Nelson, Livingston, and Stevens. They introduced themselves as Nelly, Livi, and Steve. Mr. Wooden, the draftsman, was also at the table as were the two party chiefs whom I had met the night before. Perhaps a box of divinity fudge made with pine-nuts from Mogollon which I extracted from one of my suitcases, helped toward my acceptance as a regular guy.

The location survey at the northern end of the line was almost complete so our first assignments were what might be called patch-work. I had many opportunities to display my ignorance, but I did not often make the same mistake twice.

Olancho Camp where the wind gave me part of a tent-fly for a tarp.

After a couple of weeks our two survey parties were sent to Olancha to make contour maps of the Haiwee Reservoirs. As this work at the Olancha camp neared completion, there occurred a situation in which the party chiefs, Baldwin and Hamilton, performed a major operation on my character. At the Mogollon assay office my boss, Henry Reed, was only a few years older than myself and he had practically accepted me as a companion. He had welcomed my garrulous eagerness to learn and had answered my innumerable questions and allowed me to try all the different operations so as to make me more useful.

Here, things were very different. These older men were paid to be chiefs of survey parties and were supposed to expedite the work in hand with trained men to help them. I was supposed to be a chainman but, at the time, I had never had a surveyor's tape in my hands. That, coupled with my constant readiness to put in my "two-bits-worth", must have irritated them beyond endurance.

The climax came when I was sent out with Baldwin's party to do some triangulation at several widely separated points. Baldwin carefully explained exactly what he wanted of each of the men who were assigned to the distant points. Then, as they took their departure, I waltzed up and asked him what I should do. His reply burned into my soul in a manner I shall never forget. Expurgated, it was approximately as follows: "Sit there on your back-side and keep your trap shut!" That was my first hint that I had made myself a pestiferous blight.

The pay-off came that evening when Mr. Bailey arrived with a new program which involved breaking up into three parties, each going to a different camp. Baldwin and Jones each refused to take me in their party. But Hamilton, who was to go one hundred miles down the line to Antelope Valley, volunteered to take me along as axe-man at laborer's pay of two dollars per day. I was so crestfallen and humiliated that my first thought was to pull out and go home. On the other hand, I was ashamed to be a quitter.

It was Woody, the draftsman, who saved the day for me. He privately advised me to take the new job and also to take Baldwin's advice and try to keep my mouth shut until I was spoken to. So I made a high resolve: if that was what they wanted, that was what I would do! For the next four months I do not believe that I volunteered a single remark. This, my first experience with the virtue of silence, soon won Hamilton's friendship and I was promoted to be his assistant for all odd-jobs. I slept in his tent for the rest of that assignment.

The most memorable event connected with our two months stay on this assignment at Howard's Camp in the Antelope Valley was our departure on the night of May 23rd, 1910. We were paid off when we returned from work on that day. Mr. Hamilton said that we might drive our line-wagon to Lancaster and catch the Southern Pacific "Owl" for Los Angeles at five o'clock on the morning of Tuesday, May 24th.

So, after supper we loaded our "bindles" and plenty of hay into the line-wagon and started out for Lancaster about thirty miles away over the desert. All night we cruised along under the great arched tail of Halley's comet. The crystal-clear desert air brought it out in all its regal spendor. This was a really memorable finale for the second episode of my ordeal of growing-up!

Chapter 3

WITH PROVIDENCE GENTLY GUIDING

It was only the end of May when I returned home for the second time during my "experience year". But now, college was in the offing and I made it my business in hand. I had made application to enter Cornell University in a five-year course leading to the degree of Mechanical Engineer. I had been notified by "Davy" Hoy, the Registrar, that my credits had all been accepted but I lacked three units of solid geometry. For that, I would be required to take an entrance examination after arriving at Ithaca, New York, in September. That was the real reason why I did not look for another job. I was panicked by the fear that I would cross the continent and then be turned down because of failing to pass that one crucial entrance examination.

I went to the school-book shelf in Father's library and dug out a copy of Wentworth's Solid Geometry. Upon opening it at page one, I discovered to my delight that its theorems were not as devious as I had imagined and that they soon seemed interesting and almost easy. So I spent a good deal of time studying geometry along with the usual summer activities.

And so it came about that on September 15th, 1910, I boarded the Santa Fe train for my third trip outside the State of California, bound this time for college. Father had given me a generous allowance but I immediately began to exhibit my propensity for nursing capital. I rode in a day coach all day and rented a "tourist" upper berth each night for one dollar. From Chicago, however, to Ithaca, New York, I had to travel "Pullman".

At Ithaca, then, I became a forlorn "sub-frosh" walking down the station platform. The Philadelphia-bound Delaware Lackawana and Western train began to move away and I turned my gaze very wistfully toward the emerging threshold of university life. My inclination was in accordance with the sentiments which the students insultingly attached to the initials of the D. L. & W. Railroad: "Delay-Linger-&-Wait". There was, however, no out now but to cross the platform and board the little street-car bound for the beautiful campus on the hill — "far above Cayuga's waters."

New "rushing-rules" had been imposed upon the fraternities at Cornell that year. These rules forbade a fraternity man to even look with interest at a sub-freshman after his arrival in Ithaca and before a certain hour and minute of deadline. This deadline was still about two weeks away when I took up my abode in a rooming house. Consequently I and my kind were left strictly alone except for business.

The solid geometry examination had brought me to the campus ten days ahead of registration and I was thoroughly busy until that ordeal was over. But with that safely out of the way, one would think that the following week would have been a joyful interlude with no worries and very much of interest to do and see. The very opposite was true! My misery stemmed from the only really acute attack of homesickness that I can remember in my life.

I knew that my Uncle James had written to his beloved fraternity, Sigma Phi, about my intended arrival. I had cast many furtive glances at the homelike "Sig Place" at 1½ Central Avenue on the campus. So, I made sure to be in my room on Buffalo Street as the hands of the Library clock neared seven p.m. on the appointed day.

As the clock chimed the hour, there appeared at my door a very good-looking "Sig" senior, Frank Kultchar, who had a date-card all made out for me with the first two dates at the Sigma Phi House.

After being entertained at luncheon and dinner on the first day of rushing, together with a half-dozen other rushees, I was "bid" to become a member. So, I became a "pledge" and, fortunately, never regretted my choice.

So, life at Cornell began as I was introduced to my roommate, Miller Callahan, who had been pledged the same evening with me. Each of us was surprised and pleased to find that the other knelt down to say his prayers before retiring on that memorable evening — and every evening thereafter. I have had other roommates who did not say prayers on their knees, but never one that did not show respect when I said mine.

The concept of the taken-for-granted necessity of prayer is, perhaps, the greatest spiritual endowment earned for me by my Father. And this also caused me to work hard at my Low-Church Protestant Episcopal Faith. Incidentally, this brought it about that I was popular with all the Sigma Phi freshmen during my two-year stay at Cornell, because I alone went to Church in downtown Ithaca at eight o'clock every Sunday morning.

This popularity had nothing to do with prayer; it stemmed from the fact that I thus relieved them perennially of the duty of going down to the Post Office on Sunday mornings to bring back the mail. This was no small benefit on certain Sundays later in the year when there was deep snow and the temperature was twenty-below-zero. Then, this son of "Sunny California" was welcome to plod down the hill to be present at the Communion Service at the Episcopal Church.

Along with most of the engineers, I was taking eighteen hours of studies per week. In addition, almost everyone was competing in some extracurricular activity. Mine was the freshman crew squad. This gave me the privilege of being trained by Charles E. Courtney, one of the greatest coaches of all time. When I was at Cornell, Courtney's crews had handily completed twenty-three victories without a defeat.

Weighing only one-hundred-fifty pounds, I was never promoted above the third freshman crew. But that contact with Coach Courtney was a lifelong asset, physically and manfully.

As the year ended, however, it was evident that I was not quite man enough to be a crew member. So I decided to enter the sophomore competition for business manager of the crew. This involved mostly secretarial work at the office of the Athletic Association. So I went home to Pasadena with a high resolve

My father, center, with five sons, two daughters and in-laws in the summer of 1911. I am on Father's left.

to master touch-typewriting before returning to Ithaca in September.

That summer marked the end of my boyhood intimacy with my brother Graham. He left for the Episcopalian General Theological Seminary in New York City in September. But it was while we were together that I first noticed that Graham's religious ideas were becoming different from those of the rest of the family. I had been much annoyed by his exhibition of what we called his "High-Church-antics", such as genuflecting to the altar table. I also knew that Father was much disturbed by Graham's tendency to "ape the papists", as we described his behavior. We both hoped that he would re-learn the faith of his youth when he went to the Seminary.

This hope was utterly dashed for me when I visited Graham at the Seminary in New York during my Christmas vacation from Cornell at the end of 1911. I went to Church with Graham on a weekday, but refused flatly to have any part of it. It was nothing like the kind of worship that he and I had learned together. I felt disheartened because he had departed so far from our mutual Faith. I had never seen a Catholic Mass, but this seemed to me like a repudiation of everything that the Protestant Episcopal Church stood for.

After that visit I felt that Graham and I were spiritually quite disunited. This did not, however, cause any change in my affection for him as my brother. From that time on, we had very little correspondence and I did not see him again until the summer of 1915. It was then that things had happened to make me well aware of the Catholic religion but not at all attracted to it.

I was not surprised, however, when I learned that, on May 22nd, 1912, Graham was received into the Catholic Church. In a way, I was somewhat relieved, because I thought that he was no longer masquerading but was admitting his change of faith. It was quite beyond my comprehension to understand how he had been tricked into submission to this Church. I unquestioningly regarded it as the sinister power which had, in past centuries, betrayed the precious mission of Christ.

I knew that Graham had been to France during the previous summer vacation. I wrote him a letter in which I referred to "French proselytizers" and used the adjectives "Romish" and "Popish". I do not think that there was any malice in my use of those insulting expressions. They were simply words that were familiar in the milieu in which I lived. In fact, I do remember feeling a little guilty when Graham's reply showed how he had winced under this apparent contempt expressed by his own brother. My feeling of compunction was the more genuine since his reply showed no hostility toward me.

It is really surprising to me to recall how little I ever knew about my brother's Catholic life. I knew that he entered St. Joseph Seminary at Dunwoodie, New York, in the fall of 1912. I knew that he was ordained to the priesthood on June 2nd, 1917, by Bishop Patrick Hayes at St. Patrick's Cathedral in New York. He was a guest in my home many times during the twelve years of his priesthood before his death in 1929. And yet, I know nothing about his conversion; I never saw him offer Mass or heard him preach a sermon; I never conversed with him other than very casually about religion.

Such was the spiritual "wall of separation" between the Reynolds family and this second-youngest member of it. He was, perhaps, the only member of that family in twelve generations to return to the faith which had once been almost universal in England and Wales from which his family came. His serene faith and humble yet meticulous perseverance required prodigious natural courage as well as supernatural grace by the carload!

The news of Graham's conversion brought more grief to my Father than it did to me, but his reaction was far more broad-minded than mine. He used no contemptuous language such as I had. On the contrary, he wrote to Graham and told him that he would much rather have him be a good Catholic than a bad Christian.

That busy summer of 1911 passed quickly, but when I returned to Cornell in mid-September, I had many hours of typing practice tucked away. My enthusiasm for the crew-manager competition, however, was secretly somewhat dimmed by another proposition that loomed as a possibility. It developed that the members of La Junta Club at the University of California had petitioned the Sigma Phi Society for admission as a chapter of Sigma Phi.

There were several Sigs living in the vicinity of Berkeley, California. The enthusiasm with which they praised the active members as well as the alumni of the petitioning group was very impressive.

While the discussion was going on, my enthusiasm was goaded by the intriguing notion of transferring to California in my junior year and becoming a charter member of the new chapter.

When, at last, the petition of the La Junta Club was accepted and the installation of the "Alpha of California" was definitely assured, I consulted with Father and made sure of his approval of my transfer. Then I corresponded with the Registrar of the University of California and found that my credits would be accepted for full standing as a junior in the College of Civil Engineering.

In great glee, I went to Chicago where I was to meet the two delegates from the Cornell chapter of Sigma Phi who would attend the installation of the Alpha of California, Donald Dewey, a classmate of mine, and Hamilton Allport, a budding senior. After a few blistering hot days in Chicago, we headed for California on the Fourth of July.

That summer was a short one for me because, in those days, California opened the fall term in mid-August. One event, however, was to make it stand out in my memory. My Cornell guests had neither of them ever seen a mountain before starting on this trip. So, my athletic and energetic brother-in-law, Major Fred Terrell, just returned from duty on the Mexican border, thought we ought not to stop at half-measures but should show them the best we had.

With that, we set about planning a trip over the flank of Mount Whitney. Starting from Lone Pine where I had begun my Los Angeles Aqueduct career, we would cross the divide at Cottonwood Pass, altitude eleven thousand six hundred feet, thence down Golden Trout Creek, Kern River and to Porterville.

My tenderfoot guests were a little dubious of their capacity to cope with such a mammoth project. At twenty years of age, however, one does not require much coaxing to "try anything once". Furthermore, with an experienced infantry officer along, we all felt secure so the trip was on.

The eastern escarpment of the Sierra Nevada Mountains proved to be just what it looked like from the foot — the desert turned up on edge. It was a grueling all-day climb in blistering heat. We were all exhausted when we reached Cottonwood Pass, but with Fred, the toughest of the four of us, it was more than that. He had a heart that had been trained to furnish fuel to carry him over the one-hundred-yard dash in nine and three-fifths seconds at Swathmore, ten years earlier. It had learned to demand more oxygen than it was getting now, and it was complaining of this poverty in no uncertain terms.

After a hectic night for all of us, it was decided that it would be rash for Fred to go any farther so he turned back and I was left to be the lone manager of the rest of the trip.

With that decision made, however, our troubles were ended. Ham and Don promptly became seasoned mountaineers and we spent the next two weeks in thrilling new experiences which gave Ham and Don plenty of material for casual conversation as we three took the train for Berkeley, California, on August 18th, 1912 to meet our new fraternity-brothers-to-be.

Chapter 4

A BLIND DATE DID IT

For one entering a strange university in his junior year, my position was unique. Ordinarily, one would have grave misgivings as to how he was going to fit, what new friends he would make, how to get oriented. With me it was quite the opposite. I did not know anyone in Berkeley but I felt certain that I would have a whole set of friends at the very outset. I knew that they would take care of every problem of orientation. How accurate this assurance proved to be!

Ham and Don and I had no sooner arrived in Berkeley and presented ourselves at the La Junta Club, than we were made to feel like close friends of every member of the house. This, of course, was partly an esteem given to us as symbols of the society which they looked forward to joining. But it was also due to the caliber of the men themselves which made them easy to know. The same qualities made them popular as well as influential on the campus. Our California Sigs had been well justified in their praises and hearty approval of this group of young men. They were prime candidates to be the founders of a new chapter of a fraternity with ideals of manhood and morals.

I, of course, as a new member of the group and a student at the University was taken right into the house while Ham and Don were toured about as welcome visitors and guests.

I was assigned to the long room on the third floor where I had two roommates. One was Earl Warren who was soon to graduate in Law and start on his long successful career leading to his high station as Chief Justice of the Supreme Court of the United States. My other roommate was Matt Hazeltine, a freshman who was to make his name and fame in football history.

Bill Donald, the new Graduate Manager of Athletics, was still living in the house. At a later date he would be well known

I am fourth from left at the Sigma Phi installation banquets; Earl Warren, my roommate sits at my left.

as Dr. William G. Donald, head of the University Medical staff in Berkeley.

Bill was the unwitting agent of a little event that turned out to be more important to me than any other event of my life except my birth. A few days after our arrival in Berkeley it happened that the Alpha Chi Omega Sorority was having a little party as the opener of their fall rushing program. As was usual, the rushees were invited to dinner at the sorority house. After dinner, the choicest of the boyfriends of the sorority members were invited for an informal dance.

Late in the afternoon on the day of the party, Patricia Pfitzer, the chairman of the Alpha Chi rushing committee, learned that one of the young men who had been invited was sick and could not come. So, in desperation Patty telephoned to Bill Donald who was engaged to be married to Minerva Osborn, the Alpha Chi President. Would Bill please bring along one of his brethren as substitute for the absentee! Bill replied that he had just the answer to her prayer — a Sigma Phi from Cornell who had just arrived a few days before.

Patricia, however, never having seen the young man in question, was dubious about handing him over "sight unseen" to one of her rushees. Who knows, his dancing habits might not jibe with the proprieties of local custom. Finally she said: "Well, bring him along; I'll take him myself until I see how he behaves." So, at the appointed hour, Bill and I presented ourselves at the door of the Alpha Chi house and were greeted by Minerva. She called Patricia who was upstairs with some of the rushees.

I have heard many fantastic tales about love-at-first-sight. I have always discounted them and still do. But the fact remains that the picture of Patty Pfitzer as she came down those stairs, remains as vivid in my memory as if it were yesterday instead of almost sixty years ago! The little quizzical smile on her beautiful face and the nice little dimple which was really a scar, on her right cheek made my heart turn a quiet little somersault! I secretly agreed with Bill's assurance that I would like her!

Patty's first impression of me was very much obscured by her preoccupation with the welfare of her rushees. She was, however, willing to take a second look when I telephoned to her during the week and asked if I might call at her home on the following Sunday.

It was during that week that I learned that she was a Catholic. What a sickening blow that was for me! I thought: "Why did that have to be?" If she were a cripple or an invalid, that might be cured — but if she were anything like Graham — what was the chance of a cure from Catholicism? I was badly smitten or I would have called off the date. Instead, I began to pray for her conversion. I also stepped up my own attention to my Episcopalian Faith.

Patty lived with her parents in Berkeley on the opposite side of the campus. It was not long until I was a regular caller at the Pfitzer home on Sunday afternoons.

Unknowingly, by my obvious attention to her daughter, I was seriously jeopardizing my standing with Patty's mother. She loved her daughter with intense family loyalty and could not think that anyone was good enough for her. It is almost impossible for me to associate such an idea with Mother Pfitzer. I do not think I ever knew a more docile and saintly person. Furthermore, no mother ever loved her son with greater affection than she bestowed upon me at a later date. But in the fall of 1912 it was different. When I finally declared myself to Patty at the Junior Prom in November, she was in a quandary. She did not say "No", but she felt that because of Mrs. Pfitzer's feelings, I should not come to her home any more. She also felt that I would never be happy married to a Catholic. How little did I know the depth of her faith or against what odds she was supported by the merciful grace of God.

She herself had really known nothing about the Catholic Faith until she was thirteen. It was then that she went, with several of her cousins, to live with her paternal grandmother at Santa Cruz, California. There, she attended a convent school.

The real foundation of Patty's faith, however, stemmed from the example and home teaching of this dear old matriarch from Catholic Bavaria. She had come across the plains in a prairie-schooner when Patty's father was three years old. She had done her indomitable best to raise her ten children as Catholics in the days when a priest was seldom seen in the San Joaquin Valley of California where they had settled. God in His goodness had rewarded the deep and abiding faith of "Grandma Pfitzer".

Patty's family, however, was the exception at the time. Mrs. Pfitzer was from a strictly non-Catholic family. She did not actively oppose Patty's practice of her faith but when Patty returned from Santa Cruz and entered the Berkeley public high school she had no easy time to follow what she knew to be God's will.

And now to make it still more difficult, God had allowed me to cross her path. She was beginning to love this young man in spite of the fact that my pitiful ignorance of her faith made me oppose it. If she had known how bitterly I opposed her faith, she probably would have been repelled beyond the possibility of reconciliation. Indeed, I was about as suitable for a good Catholic girl to marry as an imp of Satan.

I, on the other hand, was calmly certain that I could convince her of the simple clarity and sufficiency of my religion. Then, I thought, she would no longer be influenced by the false fear instilled into her mind by Catholic priests. If I had but known the steadfastness of her faith, without knowing more about the reason for that steadfastness, I am quite sure I would have given Patty's mother the satisfaction of knowing that I had disappeared from her life.

With these circumstances in view, it would be hard to predict anything but disaster ahead. Indeed, the outcome in the face of these circumstances is at the root of my present readiness to leave the handling of all my affairs one-hundred per cent in God's hands. It makes me thank God on my knees that only by His merciful intervention, disaster was averted in our case. Certainly,

I have never done anything, nor could I do anything to merit the outcome provided by God.

But that is ahead of my story! Patty decided that I should talk with her father and, if he approved, she would see me at the Alpha Chi house whenever house-rules would permit. So I invited Mr. Pfitzer to go with me to one of the University baseball games and we sat at the top of the grandstand and talked the situation over.

He was very kind to me and explained that his wife was not in good health at the time so it would not be well for me to come to his home. He agreed, however, that I might see his daughter provided that he always knew the circumstances. He also warned me gravely of the dangers of mixed religion in a family.

The outcome of this interview was twofold: it filled me with respect and admiration for the man who, I hoped, would one day be my father-in-law; it also confined the rest of my courtship to the walks in the vicinity of the sorority house.

Next, I wrote to my brother Graham who was at Dunwoodie Catholic Seminary, asking his advice. His reply soundly advised me to make the acquaintance of several Catholic priests and so to find out from them what I was getting into. Unfortunately, I failed to take this good advice. I did, however, exchange several letters with Graham which helped our mutual regard and also helped slightly to relieve my pitiful ignorance of the nature of Patty's faith.

And so things jogged along until shortly before the end of the college year, in May, 1913. It was then, while we were walking across the campus on the way to Patty's home, that she told me that she would marry me. We both agreed, however, that it would be after we had graduated from college. That made June, 1915, the earliest date to hope for.

That was the luckiest thing that ever happened to me! I knew that I was lucky, but sad to say, the circumstance that made it not just lucky, but luckiest, was to me the only flaw to perfect happiness.

Our dear Lord must have sighed a little to see me, not only to fail in appreciation but actually to deprecate this great gift which He was preparing for me. But He is the same Lord who made excuses for those who crucified Him — because "They know not what they do." The fact that I was unappreciative, however, does not mean that I was not supremely happy.

"That girl is one in many millions," was my sentiment, "even if she is a Catholic!"

And so I packed off to Civil Engineering Summer Camp at Santa Cruz, California, with enough enthusiasm to set the world afire and to make the rest of my college days packed with real purpose. The number of letters that passed between us must have given Mother Pfitzer a clue. But perhaps time and her improved health had helped to soften her suspicion of me. At any rate, she never complained again.

At the close of the Civil Engineering Summer Camp, I returned to Pasadena in mid-June, 1913. I was now twenty-one. Father, with his wonderful love and patience, was careful not to give evidence of hostility toward my loved one. He knew my religious views and practice and I knew his so there was no difference between us on that score. He, of course, had grave misgivings lest mixed religion would spoil the happiness of my married life. I sensed all this during the two brief months that I spent at home with Father.

My incentive to be a good engineer was now a thousandfold increased. I dug into my studies with more industry than ever before.

On November 22nd, 1913 an event occurred in the Pfitzer family which was soon to change my unhappy status as a sort of semi-outlaw. Instead, I became a welcome prospective "in-law" and practically one-of-the-family. That event was the birth of Alan Anthony Pfitzer, twenty-one years younger than Patty and about ten years younger than Joseph, Patty's other brother. Patty also had a sister, Irma, who was five years younger than Patty and a very quiet little person. So, with such an age spread,

"That girl is one in many millions."

it can be seen why Patty was a tower of strength to her mother and so much cherished by her.

With Alan's birth Mother Pfitzer's state of anxiety began to disappear and Patty rightly guessed that her attitude toward me would be greatly changed. When Patty finally summoned courage to tell her mother that she wished to marry me, it immediately seemed as if the break had never happened. From that day on, as long as she lived, Mother Pfitzer was my special booster. She was always like a second mother to me.

I never discussed religion with Patty even when we were alone together. We loved each other so much that we simply suppressed the sadness arising from incompatibility of religious ideals. It was, however, never completely out of my mind. I developed a kind of undertone of prayer which I made explicit at night. I was constantly asking God to teach me His will and give me the grace to follow it. I shall never know exactly what I meant by that prayer. I doubt if it ever occurred to me that God's will might lead me into the Catholic Church. I do believe, though, that the sincerity of that prayer made me more receptive of God's grace.

This was, of course, a very busy year for both of us. Patty was majoring in domestic science and worked at it as if she were preparing for a profession. I, too, had a heavy schedule. My transfer from Cornell to California, from mechanical engineering to civil engineering, from a five-year course to a four-year course, left me a little short of credits. This meant that I must return for the fall term, finishing in December 1914.

This gave me a carefree month at home in Pasadena, made doubly precious by a visit from Patty during the first half of July. Her gay loveliness quickly won the hearts of all the family. Llewellyn admitted that the distress he had felt when he heard that my fiancee was a Catholic, was tremendously relieved after meeting her. But how it does burn my heart to think how she must have sensed the condescension with which we all regarded her religion. How she ever put up with it is just another item of the long list of graces that God's infinite patience provided.

When we returned to Berkeley I plunged with real enthusiasm into final preparation for what I thought would be my life work as an engineering contractor. The mighty preparations then going on for the opening of the Panama Pacific Exposition in San Francisco made jobs once more easy to find. The day after my last examination in December, I went to work as "engineer" for Gutleben Brothers, San Francisco contractors, whose principal job at the moment was the construction of a model gold mine under the floor of the Palace of Mines on the Exposition grounds. The work was interesting and varied and, fortunately, this "mine" had no nitro-glycerine fumes abroad.

My work within the Exposition grounds continued long after it was open to the public. Patty also, in connection with her work in the domestic science course, was coming over twice each week to work in a domestic science exhibit which was underwritten by the University. She also had a pass to the grounds which the generous management honored on Sundays. So, like the postman on a holiday, we toured the Exposition every Sunday. This was especially precious since we did not see each other during the week.

As Patty's graduation day was approaching, I had several long visits with Father Daniel O'Kelly who was an assistant at St. Augustine's Church in Berkeley. He was only six or seven years older than myself. In the course of these talks I received my first real knowledge of what the Catholic Church claimed to be. I also learned something about the precious gifts she claimed to give to her people in the Sacraments, the Sacrifice of Mass, and the Real Presence of God on the altar. I asked Father O'Kelly how it could be possible for so many Catholics to lead lives that practically denied their belief in what their Church taught them. I had in mind one Catholic young man whom we both knew whose external life was especially scandalous who went to Mass and Communion every Sunday. His answer was that "cradle" Catholics sometimes get so used to the unimaginable blessings of their faith that they fail to appreciate its privileges.

Thirty-six years later, I sat in the sanctuary during Father O'Kelly's sermon at my first Mass in Oakland, California. Then I heard Father O'Kelly quote my objection and admit the embarrassment which the truth of my observation had cost him. But in early 1915 it passed by without my being aware of it and Father O'Kelly only advised me to redouble my fervor for my own religion. He evidently thought that my religious sincerity made it safer to hope that God would give me the grace to be open to the promptings of the Spirit. At any rate, he did not attempt a direct approach at that time.

Early in May, I received a telegram from my brother Duncan, telling me that Estelle's brother, Walter Wallace, the man who had given me my first ride in an automobile, was at the St. Francis Hotel in San Francisco and would like to see me. I stayed in town for dinner that night and went to the St. Francis Hotel to learn what next God had planned for my lucky life.

Walter had purchased an interest which made him President of two little companies manufacturing "casinghead" or natural-gasoline in the Brea Canyon Oil Field, near the little town of Brea in Orange County, California. Walter had also signed a contract with the North American Oil Company to extract the gasoline from their gas produced in the Midway Field near Taft, California.

At the time of my visit with Walter he was negotiating with several other companies for contracts to treat their gas for the extraction of its gasoline content. Most important of these was the Kern Trading and Oil Company, a subsidiary of the Southern Pacific Railroad whose "railroad-land" offered potential oil production on some sixty-nine-thousand acres. If these negotiations were successful, Walter planned to incorporate two new companies to build plants for their service.

That was the amazing set-up when I talked with Walter on that evening in May, 1915. Beside his three plants already producing natural gasoline, there was one other small plant in California. The total production of the state was about ten thousand gallons per day of this volatile fluid called "natural-gasoline".

People had not yet learned to prize it for what would come to be known as its "high octane" value.

Walter had the good judgment to know that he needed some engineering talent on his staff to face this tremendous promotion project which he was about to undertake. It took a miracle that only God could have managed, however, to direct that judgment to the selection of a freshly graduated civil engineer with no experience whatever in operating heavy machinery. But, thanks be to God, He did so direct it. Walter offered me one hundred dollars per month with a twenty-five dollar raise if I felt satisfied to make it permanent after six months trial.

Considering the billions of gallons of natural gasoline that have since passed through the California refineries, one might be tempted to say: "What luck to be twenty-three years old and be invited into the ground floor of such an industry at its very beginning!" Yes, from "hind-sight" it was indeed lucky, but from where we sat it was what oil men of that day would call a very wary "wild-cat".

The status of natural gasoline was by no means established. In fact, the recent disastrous explosion which had wrecked the town of Ardmore, Oklahoma, had given natural gasoline a bad name.

If I had been older and reasonably prudent, I never would have left a good stable job in the profession for which I was trained, to assume responsibility for the design of mechanical equipment of which I had never even seen a picture! But God had arranged every detail of this many-sided miracle to suit His plans. All I could think of was that one-hundred dollars per month would make it possible for us to be married as soon as Patty was ready.

Walter and I shook hands and it was agreed that I should report to the Superintendent of the Brea Gasoline Company on June 1st, 1915. I telephoned to Patty that night and set off in high glee next morning to break the news to Dan Gutleben and make all the arrangements for my departure. I parked my college togs and books in the Pfitzer attic, parked my Boston terrier, "Busho", with Bill and Minerva Donald who had been married the previous year-end, and said good-bye to my darling Patty on the 24th of May. That gave me one week at home before reporting for work on June 1st.

Admittedly, that seventeen-year-old who had signed on at the Los Angeles Aqueduct in 1910 was a poor excuse for a civil service chainman. But he was an expert compared with this twenty-three-year-old with a degree of Bachelor of Science in Civil Engineering, who had never handled a set of pipe-dies or been within shouting distance of an oil derrick or a gasoline plant. But here he was — too innocent to be frightened.

Fortunately, my first official job was as time-keeper so I was able to spend half my time literally burrowing into every cranny of the plants and making the acquaintance of the rest of the staff. Fortunately, too, they were all fine practical men with no engineering training, so I was given much more respect than I deserved. The result was that I was simply saturated with useful practical information every hour of every day. In addition, I visited the oil well supply houses every day and pored over their huge catalogues. I also began to help in the repair crew and learned something about pipe fitting and machine operation.

And so, ready or not, by the first of September I was sitting at a drafting board drawing plans for a gasoline plant for the newly formed Sixteen Oil Company. I was scheduled to go to Taft in the late fall as plant foreman, construction engineer and, most exciting of all, a stock holder in the new company.

This last item almost floored my Father. Each of his children had a "capital account" which accumulated from all sources. By now mine amounted to a little over five thousand dollars. I telephoned to Father and told him that Walter had invited me to invest five thousand dollars in the new gasoline plant. Father immediately sent me a half-page advertisement of the Standard Oil Company, clipped from the Los Angeles Times. This advertisement was expertly devised to extol the dangerous nature of natural gasoline. Good father that he was, however, he did not obstruct my wishes beyond that sound advice. So, once more

God's plans in my behalf moved into new territory. I became an investor in this very speculative infant industry with every dime of my principal.

All this made grist for my daily letters to Patty which were answered by her with equal enthusiasm. There was, however, one frequently repeated subject in those letters which makes me grateful to God that they have been destroyed. I set about, deliberately and determindedly to try to persuade her to renounce her Catholic Faith and marry me in the Episcopal Church. It chills my blood to think how God allowed me to become an instrument of Satan to put that crucial test before the girl I loved!

What must have been her thoughts? I shall never know. What faith she displayed! She never failed in the perfect fulfillment of all the obligations of her faith. She never even toyed with the idea of heeding my repeated plea to marry outside the Church. Yet, why was she not repelled by my blatant hostility?

There is one thing that may have saved the day for each of us — neither of us ever held back any secrets from the other. From that parting in May, 1915, until her death in 1945, we were never separated from each other without a daily exchange of letters of love and loyalty. And so that summer went into fall with me taking just enough time out for those daily letters. All else went into the design of my first natural gasoline plant for the Sixteen Oil Company. This plant was to be my particular baby for some time to come.

As the plans neared completion, my letters also began to clamor for an early date for the wedding. Finally, it was set for November 18th, since that would be the twenty-seventh anniversary for Mother and Dad. That would leave twelve days before my salary would advance to the handsome munificence of one hundred twenty-five dollars per month. Such is the optimism of youth that nothing else seemed to matter!

Chapter 5

MARRIAGE PROMOTES GOD'S PLAN

It was fortunate for me that my job was so absorbing during these last three months of my bachelorhood. I was kept busy drawing plans and reading everything I could get my hands on that was even remotely connected with natural gasoline. It all made the time pass unbelievably fast and before I knew it, Thursday, November 18th, was in the offing.

Walter Wallace had very generously suggested that I drive his beautiful Franklin coupe up to Berkeley to bring my bride home. Two days before my departure, however, a telegram from Patty read as follows: Do not bring Franklin; Dad is giving us an Overland. Imagine! a twenty-three-year-old engineer, drawing one hundred dollars per month, and the possessor of a wife and an Overland roadster! I could hardly believe that it was myself.

November 18th, 1915 was almost three years prior to the effective date of the Code of Canon Law of the Catholic Church. Our marriage was, therefore, "pre-code" and I was not asked to make or sign any of the promises that were later necessary for a valid dispensation for a mixed-marriage. I have sometimes wondered what I would have done if I had been required to sign these promises.

I have only known one young man in love with a Catholic girl who took a really consistent Protestant view of the matter. He and his fiancee came to me early in my priestly life. They were as much in love with each other as Patty and I had been. When the requirements for a dispensation to allow him to marry a Catholic girl were explained to Don, he said: "What you are asking me to do is, in effect, to sign a document admitting that her faith is true and mine is false. It would be contemptible injustice to Joan for me to do so. I love her enough to study your claim but I won't enter a half-marriage like that."

He spent almost two years after that to find the answer. As a result, their marriage was a Catholic Nuptial Mass. The happiness expressed in their later letters to me proves how perfectly right he was.

Fortunately, I did not have to face the issue in quite the same aspect so it was all a season of unadulterated joy. How could it happen that I was so lucky as to have the love of that precious person?

The wedding was to be in the living room of the Pfitzer home. That limited the number of guests to a standing room of about forty. To be honest, I could only swear as to the presence of Father O'Kelly and Patty and her father. I can see her now, as she came down the stair with her father, looking straight at me with that confidence no man could deserve. Probably less than half of those present had even seen a Catholic priest assist at a marriage ceremony. But their hearts were with us and in a very few minutes I became a married man with a wife no man could hope to deserve. And this was to be confirmed during all the rest of my life. My Father used to quote the Book of Proverbs as applied to my Mother: "Unrivaled art thou among all the women that have enriched their homes." Thank God, the same could be said of the treasure that God had given to me!

And then the fun began! Even the wedding cake was one of Mother's specialties. And all that went with it could only have been planned by one who had spent years in a college town surrounded by ravenous undergraduates.

Soon, however, Patty and I slipped away to doff dress suit and wedding gown and prepare for "going away". As she came down the stairs that time she tossed her bouquet to her double first cousin, Evelyn Pfitzer, whom I had always called "my second wife" because she was so much like Patty. Then, our family strategy began to unfold.

Our Overland had been carefully parked about a half-block down Russell Street as if all set for a secret get-away. It had, of course, been discovered and loaded down with all the atrocities of foot wear and tin cans that one might expect. We said our fond farewells midst showers of rice at the front door. Meanwhile, Dad, God bless him, had slipped out the back door and slowly driven his car out the driveway so as to cross the sidewalk just as we appeared to be making a dash for our car. We stepped in, and before any of our beloved well-wishers could transfer any of the decorations from our car, we were off to a flying start. Where were we bound? Why, to the Claremont Key Route train to take us to the Panama Pacific Exposition, of course!

What a honey of a honeymoon was ours! It lasted officially for nine days, but spiritually it is not over yet. I am confident that she is in heaven awaiting my arrival. And that is one reason why I am trying to get there. But officially, I say, it was to last nine days. The plans were drawn, the contract signed, the machinery ordered, and the crew hired. Sixteen Oil Company was getting impatient for its plant foreman.

So, we spent just two days "doing" the world's fair. We were so well acquainted with it that we knew exactly what we wanted to do and see so those two days were packed with joy. I think every honeymoon should begin with at least two days at a world's fair! Then, Saturday evening, we "went home to Mother" (and Dad).

Next morning we went to Mass together at St. Augustine's Church in Berkeley where Father O'Kelly was a curate. I can still remember how utterly blank the ceremony left me. I did not have a clue as to what was going on. The seed of grace that lay in the Sacrament of Marriage was going to be a long, long time in coming to flower.

Early that afternoon we loaded our possessions for travel into that precious Overland roadster and away we went with a hard two-day drive ahead of us. We detoured to Taft from Bakersfield because I wanted to give Patty a peek at her future home. We also wished to choose between the cottage "for free" at the Kern Trading & Oil Company camp on Section 1-C, and the house at Midway Gas Company camp which was two miles nearer to the Sixteen Oil Company plant site.

One quick look was enough to make up our minds on that problem. The house for free was a two-room box with no plumbing and no porch. The Midway house, aside from being closer to the job, was a lovely four-room cottage with a bath and a wide screen porch all around. Fifteen dollars per month was the rent and that would still leave ten dollars out of the increase we were expecting next month. And then, a good T-bone steak for two could be had for twenty-five cents at Sol Coleman's store in Taft.

That decision made, we dashed over to the plant-site and then back to the Midway Gasoline Company camp where we were cordially welcomed by Dick Bergston, the foreman, and his wife Bertha. That must have helped Patty to down her somewhat anxious thoughts at the prospect of making a home in this tawny and treeless desert. It was saved from being also trackless only by a sparse orchard of oil well derricks, set out in rows to be sure, but giving a fragrance far different from the orange-blossom-scented airs of Sunny Southern California.

The only part of that poetic epithet which prevailed here was accent on the sun, plus wind and dust. But how quickly other circumstances can obliterate the bitter taste of temporal surroundings! It would be "home" for us, and what a fascinating home it was! An ideal place for married life to find a firm foundation, where each to the other meant all.

Pioneering, problem solving, proving worth, both in love and in work. It would not be long till every return to the oil fields through the "Gap" at Section 36 would bring to each of us a sigh of contentment as we inhaled the typical oil field air which to an outsider smells tainted but to us meant home and its promise of success.

But now we were off again for three days more of honeymoon at Pasadena before our great adventure was to begin. We ate our picnic lunch, as we were to do many, many times in the days to come, just where we happened to be at noontime. This time it was a most prosaic spot, under a Joshua tree in the Antelope

Valley. For us, however, it had a special attraction because we could look down along the line of that five-mile-long Neenach Siphon of the Los Angeles Aqueduct. It was there that I finished my last day's work as rear-flag on a survey party just five years earlier. How little had I dreamed on that day, of the happiness of my next visit.

Then, on we went, down Bouquet Canyon into Saugus and San Fernando and pulled up the driveway at 257 West California Street just in time for late supper with Father and Margaret.

After three days we set out for our new home at Taft. There we found that good Dick Bergston had deposited Patty's trunk and box of wedding presents and a bed at our house at the Midway Gas camp. It was fortunate that a trunk shipped by freight had to be enclosed in a wooden box. That box was our dining table for some weeks while I plunged into our great new adventure in oilfield pioneering with all my five-month background of experience. Whatever else might be said of this hopeful young couple, there could be no doubt that we were "starting from scratch" to fulfill our respective roles.

In 1915 the "process" for extracting gasoline from natural gas was a fairly simple operation. The "Saybolt" patents held by one of the Standard Oil group, stood in the way of any outsider who flirted with the idea of using a neutral oil to absorb gasoline vapor from the gas and recover it by ordinary distillation. Consequently, the only other method available, and the one universally used, was to compress the gas and then cool it, thus condensing the gasoline vapor just as water vapor is condensed into rain.

The gas coming from the earth with the crude petroleum was separated from the oil in a gas-trap located at the well. It was then sucked into the gasoline plant under vacuum or low pressure and compressed to two or three hundred pounds per square inch. The compressed gas was then cooled, first by water spray, then by using the gas itself to drive an ordinary steam engine. The cold exhaust was used to chill the incoming gas to the engine. The resultant temperature was about forty degrees below zero Fahrenheit. This liquefied all of the gasoline vapor in the gas and even liquefied some of the heavier constituents of the gas itself.

I shudder, though, to recall those early operations. No one seemed to think that it was risky to expand the compressed gas through a steam engine designed to be driven by steam at one hundred pounds per square inch, and not gas at forty below zero and two hundred fifty pounds per square inch! Anyway, they did not fly to pieces — often — and they really did squeeze out all the gasoline.

The term "high octane" had not been invented in those days, but it would have only mildly described the product that came out of our condensers at this high pressure and low temperature.

But before all this could happen at the plant of the Sixteen Oil Company, there was much hard work to be done and I was the one elected to see it through. So, leaving Patty to keep house with our very few possessions, I started out bright and early on Monday, November 29th, with four mules, two Fresno scrapers, and five men to excavate the site for the new engine room, cooling towers, and storage tanks. We had our troubles from day to day but the men were always loyal to the job in those days. Furthermore, they seemed to credit me with more knowledge than I really had. One thing that helped — my appearance did not betray my youth.

Three events stand out in memory during those first months on Section Sixteen: the arrival of the first gas engine, the "Big Wind", and a thunderstorm.

The arrival and installation of our first big power unit has a reminder for me in these present days. It was a two-hundred horsepower stationary gas engine. It was loaded on a flatcar at the factory and because of its fourteen tons of solid weight, it was not even placed upon cleats. So, when it came time to unload it, we had first to drive wedges under its great bulk of cast iron to pry it up enough to get rollers under it. Then we gradually nursed it over onto a trailer with steel tires twelve inches wide. Then, with two trucks in tandem, it was towed up

The site of the Sixteen Plant, December, 1915.

the long hill to the plant. Another half day was required to unload it onto the foundation block. So it took almost two days of work for six men and two trucks to move that chunk of cast iron three miles. I think of that in these days whenever I see a hundred-ton jet liner sail down a runway and take off into the air at several hundred miles per hour!

The Big-Wind was almost unique. It happened in March, 1916. It was the very day that the first unit of the plant was ready for operation. The compressor, with a driving pulley eight feet in diameter, was driven by a belt from the gas engine thirty-two feet away. The belt was eighteen inches wide and one half inch thick and was very tough. But even with a light load on the compressor, the new belt soon stretched enough to sag considerably.

At about 1:30 p.m., almost without any warning, a gust of wind whirled through the open end of the unfinished engineroom and whipped that heavy belt off the pulleys as if it had been a ribbon of tinsel. The engine was immediately shut down and then things began to happen! The first few gusts were quickly followed by a howling seventy-mile-an-hour gale. Half of the engine-room roof was ripped off and went sailing out of sight over the hill. All hands grabbed shovels and began piling sand into cement sacks to hold tight the guy wires on the cooling tower.

We concentrated our efforts on the big tower since the gas pipes were already under pressure. We were successful in saving this important part of the plant. Before we finished that job, however, the wind had made jack-straws out of the engine cooling tower. The engine-room itself was now fairly safe since the yawning hole in the roof let the wind out as fast as it came in. So, nothing else remained to be done except look out for our own safety.

The gale in our vicinity was beginning to be laden with much that was not air. Every now and then a swirling crazy sheet of corrugated iron roofing would go end-over-end up our hill. Then there would be bevies of shingles. We decided to take refuge behind a ten-thousand-barrel water tank which stood on top of the hill back of the plant. No sooner were we huddled there, than the wind pressure caused the brim-full tank to overflow and drench us with a copious deluge. So, we crawled into the next-best place — facing into the eye of the wind in front of the tank.

Here we could at least see and dodge any air-borne missiles that came our way. We soon noticed that each of us was taking on a quite unnatural brownish complexion. It was not long until we were made aware of the cause. The air was gradually taking on the production of many of the flowing wells in the vicinity! The wind shook the wooden derricks to such an extent that their many guy wires could no longer keep them standing. As they crashed to the ground, the "Christmas-Tree" of valves at the top of the well casing was broken off and the finely atomized oil took to the wind.

We crouched in this precarious but highly spectacular vantage point from 2:30 p.m. until nearly five o'clock. Then the wind subsided almost as quickly as it had begun. During this time we had seen six nearby derricks collapse. We learned later that fourteen hundred derricks fell in the entire area, as well as many bunk houses and other small buildings. I knew that our house over at Midway headquarters was well built, but I did some of the most anxious praying of my life, as of then, that my darling wife would not be injured.

As soon as, or perhaps a little sooner than, it was less than foolhardy to attempt to drive a car over the road, I cranked up the Model T Ford which was my "Company Car". I then threaded my way on and off the road, avoiding debris and guy wires of collapsed derricks until, with a sigh of relief, I could see that all the cottages at our camp were still standing. In fact, our house was so well built that Patty, bless her heart, had not realized that there was much danger. She admitted that she had thought with satisfaction that it was a good thing that I was up at the plant so that I could see that nothing went wrong on account of the Big-Wind!

She was, however, wide eyed with astonishment the next day when she saw the havoc that I had been through. And so began that complex of danger and joy and achievement which always accompanies pioneering out on the frontier of any enterprise. It not only knit husband and wife into a powerful team of admiration, respect, and love, but it did the same between us and the other young people whom we quickly came to know. Friends meant much more in the oil fields than elsewhere and we thought nothing of visiting back and forth over many miles of very rough roads.

After a month of hurried repair, the plant was again ready for operation and, this time, for production too. The first two months were a bit rugged for me since the first two units did not justify hiring an extra crew for operation. Construction went merrily on until four more units were added to the plant. So, as foreman, I came on the job at 7:30 a.m., and, as engineer running afternoon tour, I was free to go home at midnight.

Usually Patty would load a basket with supper and drive over to the plant and sometimes stay until midnight. She was always accompanied by that only child of ours, Busho, the Boston Terrier. He was a clown if there ever was one! Thus it happened that Patty and Busho were at the plant on the night of the big thunderstorm. It started with a deluge of rain for about an hour before the lightning began.

Now, Busho had never signed on as a hunting dog and, in spite of his bluff at bravery most of the time, he admitted that he was utterly terrified at any kind of a sharp report. On this occasion it was not long until there was a blinding flash followed almost immediately by a roar of thunder that even made my hair bristle a little. With that, Busho hurled himself out of the car and dashed out into the darkness for keeps.

When midnight came the storm was well over, but no Busho appeared. So, there was nothing to do but return over the still watery two miles of road to the house. I opened the door of the screen porch and there was Busho. He had seen the car drive up and came to meet us registering shame more effectively than I ever saw it done by a human being.

Eyes brimming with tears, he fairly groveled on the floor in anticipation of being flayed alive when we had learned the cause of his shame. He had apparently never stopped running after leaving the plant. In his flight through dark he had plowed through several rivulets laden with drops of the blackest of waste oil. In this condition he had pushed open the door of our bedroom and had crawled in *between the sheets!* I wish to place it on record, however, that I did not punish him. He had already suffered an agony of fear. And I remember that I was a lot older than he was before I myself learned to overcome the fear of lightning.

But I must get on with the fabulous story of our adventure in this new industry. The short history of the Sixteen Oil Company followed a pattern which was to become classic. Starting on a "shoestring" with only enough gas in sight to give a "hope for tomorrow", it quickly built up as more wells were drilled, more contracts signed, more units added. At no time, however, was it anything but risky business depending on many variables.

One of these variables arranged by God was not on the schedule. As June merged into July, 1916, I began to be very much annoyed with myself because I seemed to be wilting under the hot weather. Every evening I could come home exhausted from an ordinary day's work. About twice a week I brought home a fifty-pound cake of ice made at the plant in a can packed within the insulation of our high-stage cooler. This little block of ice was always the same size, but each time it seemed heavier as I lifted it into the ice-compartment at the top of our refrigerator. It fitted into the box almost exactly, with less than a half inch to spare at either end. There came a time in mid-July when I gave a mighty heave to lift it to the top of the box. It promptly settled an inch or two into the ice compartment wedging my fingers securely against the ends of the box. With my hands locked at shoulder height, I was unable to do anything but shout to Patty for help. She instantly sized up the situation, grabbed the ice pick and with twice her natural strength, hacked at the end of the block until a large chunk broke off and set me free.

With that, I staggered along the screen porch to the open French doors of the bedroom and collapsed in a faint on the bed. Once more Patty was the valiant wife described in the Book of Proverbs. "The man who has found her has found a rare treasure brought from distant shores. Bound to her in loving confidence, he will have no need of spoil. Content, not sorrow, she will bring to him as long as life lasts."

Patty remembered enough first-aid to bring me back to consciousness and then went to the Gas Company office to call a doctor. When the doctor arrived he assured Patty that I was doing pretty well to hold my temperature to only 103° when the temperature outside was 114°. He suspected correctly that I had been trying to prove that I could walk out of a case of typhoid fever. That fifty-pound block of ice had slapped me down just in time to avoid serious consequences. The doctor also insisted that I should be taken to a hospital in a place less torrid than Taft.

In that brief order for my welfare, the doctor, quite unknowingly, caused the beginning of a bond which forever cemented the mutual love and loyalty between Patty's parents and their son-in-law. It was to bear abundant fruit and perhaps many spiritual graces in later days.

As soon as the doctor had left, Patty went again to the Company office and telephoned to her father in Berkeley.

Chapter 6

MUCH BUSINESS AND MUCH ELSE

In 1916 a long-distance telephone call was more of an event than it is in these days of Direct Distance Dialing. So, this was the first time Patty had called her home. The fact that she called her father and not her mother also gave a hint that there was an emergency. And so her message brought immediate action in the Pfitzer household. Patty returned to tell me with grateful relief that Mother and Dad were on their way to the rescue. Driving most of the night, they arrived in the wee small hours of the morning. Then, after giving them a couple of hours for sleep, we set forth for Pasadena.

Dad's old Studebaker served admirably as an ambulance. With the "bucket" front seat removed, I was stretched out on a mattress laid on the floor while the other three sat tandem on the driver's side. Our early morning start made it possible to avoid the worst of the desert heat, but it was an exceedingly tired foursome that arrived at my father's house in Pasadena in mid-afternoon on July 14th.

After a good night's sleep for all of us, I was taken to the Pasadena Hospital where I improved so rapidly that I was able to return to Father's house after only five days. I remained there for another two weeks, then, after three weeks in Berkeley, I was in shape to go to work again and soon forgot the languor of the early summer.

In November came a history-making announcement. It was decided to place all continuous operations on a basis of three eight-hour shifts instead of the traditional twelve-hour tour. The change was scheduled to take effect as of January 1st, 1917. This required some maneuvering of accommodations and personnel so it was decided that I should go to the Los Angeles office for the last month of 1916. This gave us a happy Christmas in Pasadena with the family.

On December 28th, in order to be sure to be on hand in plenty of time for the three-shift changeover, we left immediately after lunch in spite of the threatening stormy weather. All went well as we coasted down from the Ridge Route into the Antelope Valley. Even so, a quiet fall of snow had covered the road about four inches deep. As we approached Bailey's Ranch a gust of wind whipped quite a powdering of snow across the windshield of our trusty Overland.

I said to Patty, "What do you think — should we stop at Bailey's and wait till morning?"

"Oh", she said, "it's only about five miles to the summit of Grapevine Canyon and from there we are as good as home!"

"O.K.", I said, "Let's go!"

We were less than a mile past Bailey's when the wind whipped up into a gale from the south. Being at our back, we did not realize at first how strong it was. We were, however, able to keep going and by watching out for the rapidly forming drifts, I had almost reached the summit when a stage going fast in the opposite direction came around a curve close ahead of us. My only chance to avoid a collision was to turn aside into a nice fluffy snowdrift about two feet deep.

We had scarcely stopped when another car stalled in the same drift directly behind us. The occupants, another young couple, were climbing out when a second stage pulled up behind the one which had caused us to stall. The driver of the first stage opened the door. I grabbed Busho out of our car and shoved him into Patty's arms as the two ladies climbed aboard. With that, the door slammed shut and the driver of the second stage yelled to us to hurry up. There was no time to waste, so we two husbands reluctantly got aboard the second stage containing only one passenger and a burly driver who was more than partly drunk.

My heart sank as this driver, shouting, "It's Los Angeles or bust," gave his steering wheel a mighty heave and, pulling his stage around and ahead of the other one, dashed off leaving them out of sight in the growing dusk. It was almost dark by the time he had maneuvered his big stage back over the four miles to Bailey's Ranch and let us out while he disappeared again into the night.

We waited in frantic fear for almost an hour while the wind and snow increased in violence. I tried in vain to get the proprietor to hitch his team to a sled and go back in search of the missing stage. Finally, he gave us a lantern and many burlap sacks to wrap the ladies' feet in lieu of snowshoes and we started out on foot.

After walking almost three miles with the gale blowing at our backs, we came upon a long hill — down grade for us — but enough up-grade to have stalled about a dozen south-bound cars. Among them, to our tremendous relief, was the half-ditched stage containing our wives and six men. They were all thoroughly cold in spite of the warmth supplied by the motor which had been kept running.

We had long since discovered that it was hopeless to try to walk south toward Bailey's Ranch against the gale. But all were ready to make a try for shelter in a school house a couple of miles to the north. With that, the driver shut off the motor, drained the radiator, and the ten of us started off on foot headed north.

We had no sooner passed beyond the headlights of the last stalled car than the folly of our quest became apparent. Even the fences at the side of the highway were now covered in many places with drifting snow. One man decided to try it alone. He took the lantern and the rest of us, now nine in number plus Busho, returned to the listing stagecoach and prepared to face a bitter struggle against the temptation to fall asleep and freeze.

All that night the wind howled and finely powdered snow, not very much above zero in temperature, sifted through the cracks in the battered side curtains. There was an illuminated clock on the dash and it was first class torture to sit and watch it. Several times I would have sworn that the pesky thing had stopped, but it kept ticking away in derision.

Talking and jiggling our feet helped to keep us awake, but I did a lot of thinking that night that I did not make vocal. This was the same desert valley that I had lived in seven years before while working on the Los Angeles Aqueduct. I had seen such storms blow for three days on end. It was the first time I had ever faced a real valid possibility of death. Since our marriage I had been so frantically busy that I had given almost no thought to God's thoughts about me. But that night was different. Time to think was what we had in plenty and I don't mind saying that I was scared.

In the wee small hours of the morning, when the temptation to sleep was almost overpowering, I made a promise to God in a sort of embarrassed way. I said in my heart that if He got us out of this in safety, I would really try to learn the truth about the Catholic Church. It seems strange, too, that I put it that way, because I certainly had no notion then of *joining* the Catholic Church.

All this made a perfect providential setting. Looking back at it now, it seems so obvious. Everything clicked so perfectly and with such split-second timing. Our decision not to stop at Bailey's Ranch — exactly the right amount of snow—exactly the right time of day— exactly the right amount of wind — the other car stalled just behind ours. Except for the other woman, Patty and I never would have been separated. The two stages, one with only two vacant seats and an unsure driver, the other lightly loaded with the driver rather drunk. The drained radiator — the guiding fences covered with snow — the long, cold, windy night. All these, precisely meshed by the Providence of God, brought their impact upon the lives of each of the nine occupants of that stage.

Then God answered my proposal. Daylight brought a perfect calm clear day. How little I thought of my part of the bargain! It terrifies me to realize how thoughtlessly I set aside the grace which God's goodness offered me. I let the thorns of a busy life choke the impulse — so clearly a gift from God, for thirteen long years. How could I fail to see it?

At dawn our hill presented a comic sight with a dozen automobiles at various angles strung along like sitting ducks, up to their hubs in snow. The joy of calm daylight was soon immensely increased when a group of highway engineers from Bailey's Ranch appeared on the scene. They had tramped down the snow to make a semblance of a trail that the ladies could navigate with our help. We started out on foot and reached Bailey's Ranch about mid-morning. There we reveled in a great platter of bacon and eggs and other fresh ranch edibles.

Late the second afternoon we thawed out the Overland and made our way to Taft with one day to spare before the inauguration of the three-shift-eight-hour-day at the Sixteen Oil Company plant. This soon smoothed things out in many ways.

The eight-hour-day was not the only innovation in the spring of 1917. Walter Wallace had promoted a merger of all the plants into one new corporation to be called Wallace Refineries. My stock was exchanged for twice the number of shares of the new company and began to pay a nice little dividend much to my father's relief.

I was appointed "Chemist" of Wallace Refineries and moved my activities to the "Laboratory" at the Puritan Plant. There I worked with two young engineers, Charles F. Bevan, and James K. Wilson. Our main project was the design of a pilot oil-absorption plant to try out the new process when the Saybolt patents were abandoned. When it was put in operation in May, 1917, Charlie and Jim departed for the mid-continent and thence to service in World War One.

And, speaking of World War One, my name was called in the very first draft but the medical examiners turned me down — you would never guess why! — flat feet. Those flat feet have painlessly carried me over more miles of hiking than ever would have been required in the war. But, quite obviously, God had other plans — and flat feet suited His purpose well.

My work was now centered at the main office, so I was moved into a cottage at the "35-B Booster" about a mile from the office. The long brown slope up to this cottage would never impress

The little lawn at the 35B Cottage brings memories

one as a site to promote the budding career of a couple of garden lovers, but that is exactly what happened. Parched anemic soil to the contrary notwithstanding, we were soon on our way. We had a little lawn about twelve feet square in front of the house. It was flanked by a small row of iris that grew more luxuriantly than any others I have seen. They evidently had exactly what it takes to make iris thrive.

The luxury of that little lawn was impressed on my memory by a few words that passed between Patty and myself while we lay in the middle of it looking up at the millions of stars on a hot summer night. The stars started me talking about God and that led to the mention of the divinity of Christ and the founding of His Church. I cannot remember Patty's exact words but the thought burned into my soul and nagged me for an answer until God suggested the only consistent one fourteen years later.

Patty simply asked how any Church beside the Catholic Church could be the one founded by Christ, since it was the only one that had been in existence since the time of Christ. My answer that the corrupt hierarchy of the sixteenth century had betrayed the people, did not seem very convincing in the face of Christ's promise that that was exactly what would *not* happen. It occurred to me that if it *had* happened, the "Gates of Hell" had certainly "prevailed". And how could that be reconciled with the belief that Christ is God? I did not, however, voice these thoughts. Instead, I put them aside as I was to do many times in the future. I left it at the uneasy conclusion that competent Protestant theologians must have considered that there was a sufficient answer.

Soon after that evening I nursed Patty through a siege of well-named "yellow jaundice". As she began to feel better, she took a look at herself in a mirror and decided that if my love could survive such a shock, she was safe for life "in sickness and in health".

While I was nursing Patty's jaundice, people everywhere began talking about the epidemic of "Spanish Influenza" making its appearance in various places. My dear father took to his bed in July. His Parkinson's disease had reduced him to a very crippled state and probably lowered his resistance to the influenza. As soon as Patty was well, we went to Pasadena and found him quite chipper but still in bed. I had to return to Taft in mid-August, but early in September his condition worsened and turned into pneumonia. Jessie sent word to me to come immediately, but he died a few hours before I could be there to kneel at his bedside on Thursday, September 5th, 1918.

He was a Protestant in good faith if external evidence means anything at all. I doubt if it had ever occurred to him to think of the apparent inconsistency which was bothering me. If he did, he contrived a better answer than mine. He was so forthright that no human respect would ever have held him back from going to the very bottom of the question.

Patty and I returned to Taft and resumed "business as usual". It was not long, however, until cases of "flu" began to appear in our midst. By the end of October we were a part of the epidemic area. The whole community took to gauze masks and serum. Those who remained on their feet went about with considerable anxiety because no one seemed to be able to tell us how the disease was communicated.

Soon, all the schools were closed and the new high school building was converted into a hospital with eighty beds. Patty, with her knowledge of dietetics volunteered her services and was immediately installed as cook. I drove truck and served as general handy-man. The first part of November was very grim. Patients were dying at the rate of three or four every day and the volunteer workers were becoming vulnerable through fatigue.

On November 11th, however, the tremendous news that the "war-to-end-war" was over, seemed to give an immunizing fillip to the whole community. The flow of in-patients tapered off to almost nothing. Before November was over, the little local hospital was adequate for all the new cases and soon the high school, after elaborate fumigation, was reopened. By Christmas time we felt safe in going to Berkeley to enjoy the day with Patty's family.

In February, 1919, Walter Wallace began to have ideas of expansion into the many booming oil fields of the midcontinent, so he sent me on a six-weeks sally into Texas and Oklahoma. I found the field well combed and the royalties offered were much higher than any that we paid in California. So, I returned to Taft at the end of March, wiser and well satisfied to confine our expansion to California. Indeed, the California oil fields furnished plenty of opportunity for expansion.

All this kept me more than occupied as Chemist and Plant Designer, but it got really formidable when I became Field Superintendent on September 1st, 1919. How relieved Father would have been as the financial situation began to shape up. It soon made my original venture of five thousand dollars look very small. From first to last, however, it involved a risk that would have been unpalatable to Father personally.

As plants and production increased, new business and new contracts began to be available to us almost for the asking. What a tremendous experience it was! Walter Wallace was constantly pushing me into more and more responsibility and complaining that I should be at least ten years older. Somehow, the calendar would not do anything to remedy that defect.

Finally, in November, 1920, an event occurred which changed all this for us. A promising offer came to Walter Wallace for a gasoline plant in the roaring new field of Breckenridge, Texas. I was sent to look it over; reported favorably; and had it land in my lap!

And so, it was not without keen regret that Patty and I parked our belongings in the Wallace Refineries warehouse at Taft and drove away on December 1st, 1920, after five years and three days of residence.

The experience of these five years made it hard to leave and the prospect at Breckenridge was indeed rough-and-tumble. By that time, however, I felt like a seasoned "oil man" and Patty and I had become a team with untold confidence in each other. The picture was not dampened, I must admit, by the new assignment as Assistant Manager of Wallace & Brooks, Inc., of Breckenridge, Texas, with a salary of ten thousand dollars per year which, in 1920, jingled as musically as would thirty thousand today.

Chapter 7

THE BATTLE OF BRECKENRIDGE

If "challenge" means: encounter with problems and people and events without recourse to an immediate "backer" — then I am sure that what Charlie Bevan and I always called "The Battle of Breckenridge" was the greatest challenge of my life. That statement, however, needs immediate qualification in several directions.

It startles me a little to recall that the first and all-sufficient Backer with Whom I am now prepared to meet any and every challenge, as of today, never entered into my calculations as a Partner.

Of visible backers, however, the most obvious qualification I must admit, appears in the person of our resident Vice President, the genial and diplomatic Charles W. Brooks who had promoted the entire project. He was a typical Southerner, equipped to mitigate all the varied conflicting influences of an oil-boom-town in the Texas "sticks". Without him or his equivalent, a Yankee would never have made first base in that ball game.

His backing was, of course, an absolute necessity for success. So was that of Charlie Bevan whom I contacted by mail as soon as Wallace and Brooks was a certainty. Charlie had returned to the Oklahoma oil fields at the close of the war, but he joyfully signed on as my assistant for "the duration". The backing of my Patty was also a necessity. But what I mean about the uniqueness of this challenge stems from my status in the project. It was the first and only time that I found myself set down on the edge of a nice flat patch of "grass roots" as the sole operating boss. Among those grass roots, I was to conjure a million dollar plant to gather and treat the gas from madly drilling wells in every direction.

"I was to conjure a million dollar plant to gather and treat the gas from madly drilling wells in every direction."

I would be terrified to undertake such a project now. But on the morning of December 6th, 1920, there was nothing but thrilled enthusiasm in my heart as I boarded the antiquated passenger coach at Cisco, Texas, bound for Breckenridge.

Prolonged torrential rains made quite an event of the twenty-eight mile trip to Breckenridge. I was cooled off a little as the train slowed down to a slow walk while crossing a high fill. I had a hint as to the reason for the reduced speed as the coach heeled over perilously with me on the "downside". This hint was clinched a hundred feet further along when five box cars came into view at the bottom of the fill with great gouges in the bank where they had rolled down.

A further dampening of ardor came when the train reached Breckenridge and I put my foot down a prodigious distance, not onto a station platform, but into ankle-deep mud.

And then began "The Battle of Breckenridge".

It was really an amazing privilege for a twenty-eight-year-old engineer to have placed in his lap. My instructions were: "Build a gasoline plant to treat all the gas that Charlie Brooks has contracted for."

By 1920, the extraction of natural gasoline by compression and refrigeration was obsolete. A "natural gasoline plant" meant an oil-absorption plant such as I had been building with Charlie Bevan and Jim Wilson in California but on a very much larger scale. The physics of the process is quite simple, but it was surprising the number of "firsts" we had to meet.

The problems of pioneering in new construction, however, were not what made it "The Battle of Breckenridge". Part of the battle element was, of course, generated by the mad scramble for every conceivable kind of material and service. But the main element was new to me and gave me a real shock. It was the universal hostility against "Yankees".

Wallace and Brooks had no roots other than California but we were somehow ranked as a "Yankee" outfit. If it had not been for Charlie Brooks, we would have come out second best in every item of competition for service, material, and even the fulfillment of promised commitments. The Civil War was fifty-five years back in history, but too often, when I opened my mouth and did not produce that comfortable Texas accent, the air seemed to be tainted with the odor of black powder and flintlocks. It was never voiced as hatred against me personally, but it was always "open season" for Yankees.

One amusing misfire of Yankee-baiting occurred in the deal for our very first carload of gasoline sold. It happened that it was purchased through a local sales agency and shipped to a refinery at Coalinga, California, about eighty miles from our main office at Taft. When this car arrived at Coalinga, the following telegram came from the agent: "Carload gasoline refused acceptance; product off-color; advise disposal." I wired back: "Hold for arrival of our chemist from Taft to take sample." The reply: "Car unloaded by mistake — accepted", spoke for itself.

The sale of this first carload of our product recalls the unpromising situation which finally led to our disposal of the Texas venture. When I arrived in Breckenridge, our California product was selling at twenty-seven cents per gallon. This, our first delivery from Texas, sold for six cents per gallon. The depression of 1921 affected the oil industry early. And so it came about that our Breckenridge plant was finally taken over by Chestnut and Smith whose extensive mid-continent operations gave them status for doing business and meeting difficulties which corresponded with ours in California. Since they were ready to take over the entire project at par value, we were quite ready to withdraw.

The Battle of Breckenridge, however, has stored my memory with a strange little kaleidoscope of experiences which I now see had their place in the mosaic of life that God was designing for me. It taughtmemuch about things and people.

There was an unassuming little man in blue-jeans who used to drop in at the office quite frequently, apparently just looking for company, and thoroughly unhappy. It turned out that he was the owner of a rather large cattle ranch nearby. This ranch had supported him and his wife and son and daughter at little more than starvation level during the previous three years of drought. Unlike many of his neighbors, instead of selling outright to the oil prospectors, he had chosen a favorable royalty contract. As a result, while oil was selling at $3.75 per barrel, he was briefly in possession of an income of several hundred thousand per year.

As a sequel, however, when I first met him, his son was in an institution for alcoholics and his wife and daughter had left with strange men for the bright lights of the big city. He lived on alone, batching in the old farm house now surrounded by flowing oil wells.

Another similar blue-jeaned land owner was in a much happier state of mind. He, too, had continued to live in the old farm house with his family. When the third gusher came into production on his land, our pipeline crew arrived to install a gas trap and make connections into our gathering line. The farmer asked our pipeline foreman if he was going to return to the oil company's office.

"I belong to Wallace and Brooks," he replied, "but I can stop by and leave a message for you."

His message was this: "The lease man told me that I would be gettin' pay for this oil within a month after the first well came in. I been waitin' four months now and I'm out of funds and I owe about fifty dollars at the store. I wish you'd ask 'em to advance me a little money. I need it right bad."

"Haven't you received any royalty checks by mail?" asked Frank in amazement.

"No. They send a statement each month, but no money."

With a sly smile, Frank asked to see the "statements" and walked with him over to the house. There, from a jar on the top shelf in the kitchen, there emerged three statement-checks totaling more than fifty thousand dollars.

Another experience involved money, but on a much smaller scale. As the 1921 depression waxed in proportions, anyone with money to spend became an item of interest to an increasing number of people quite without regard to Yankee accent. One of these attracted to our office was a free-lance salesman of oil-field equipment. Most of our buying was on a large enough scale to be of interest to manufacturer's agents so I had never placed any orders with this individual. In any case, there was something about him that I just didn't cotton to.

One noon when I came back to my desk in the office, there was a sealed envelope addressed in pencil: "For the engineer" — and that was all. It contained seventy-five dollars in crisp new bills — nothing else. At first, I was nonplussed as to how to handle this one. On second thought, however, I made a little silent thanksgiving that Charlie Brooks was in his office. I took the envelope in and laid it on his desk. He picked it up, surveyed its contents and address, then put it down. Neither of us spoke but his pleasant smile told me a page-full as he slipped the envelope in his top drawer. So, I very gratefully went about my business at the plant.

When I returned a few hours later, Charlie was gone but Bob, the bookkeeper who bunked in the office, was still there and he was beside himself with glee. Our friend had called and Charlie had received him with the warm Southern cordiality of which he was a past master. Remember, Charlie had absolutely nothing that would enable him to pin it on this man. One misstep would have fouled up the whole encounter. Charlie's only advantage was that the other man was ignorant of the presence of the envelope in Charlie's top drawer.

Charlie invited him into his office and closed the door so Bob was not able to report the preamble. Secretly, I would have given the seventy-five dollars to have had a tape-record of Charlie's smiling gracious suavity as he gradually became dead sure of his quarry. Then, still in a very gracious tone, Bob began to hear nouns and adjectives and a verb or two that made it quite clear that the expression on the stranger's white face would not be one of joy as he opened the door and fairly oozed himself backwards down the steps and out into no-man's land, never to be seen again.

I cannot leave the story of the Battle of Breckenridge without one more tribute to my precious wife and a salute to Charlie Bevan's bride. Lyda Bevan arrived when things were just a little bit less rugged, but she helped on many occasions to save the day for all of us.

What thrills me with admiration is the perfection with which Patty made it appear to me that she entered into all this pioneering without finding it a trial. Indeed, her loyalty and the sense of team identity between us did remove the sting of many trials. I had the thrill of professional achievement to mitigate the disappointments, but Patty had to live with them all day long. Of course, that too had its character of professional achievement in what, today, I would call her "Project Sainthood".

She arrived in Breckenridge on December 31st, 1920, and moved in with Charlie and me to occupy two little rooms at the back of our first temporary office hut. The "bathroom" was a wooden trough on the roofless porch, supplied with a bucket of water each day from the plant. Our meals for the first few days were provided by another "valiant woman" "Ma" Thompson, who ran the town restaurant a mile away to the west.

Fortunately, we soon moved into our not-quite-finished house on the Quakins Petroleum property where our plant was being built. There, we had a bath-tub in which one could well imagine himself bathing in strong tea. That was the permanent color of the water brought by pipeline from the Brazos River twelve miles away. Our drinking water was condensed steam from the boiler room.

Patty, whose grandparents on one side had crossed the plains in a "prairie-schooner", and on the other side had come around the Horn in a sailing vessel, always claimed that she did not inherit their pioneering instinct. Her behavior in this new life, however, belied her claim. She always made the best of every situation as each one came along.

She never even gave me a clue as to what it cost her to be almost entirely separated from the Church and the Sacraments. The Catholic population of that part of Texas was almost nil. A priest visited Breckenridge a few times each year to take care of the needs of the faithful-few who came together from miles around. How they knew when he was coming or where Mass was to be celebrated, I have not the faintest idea. I am ashamed to admit that I never went to Mass with Patty and never saw a priest during our stay in Breckenridge. She, however, was always uncomplaining.

In fact, it was not until twenty-one years after Patty's death that Lyda Bevan, helping me to sharpen memories about Patty and Charlie at Breckenridge, wrote in a letter:

"I can recall only one time that Patty expressed her feelings about the Battle of Breckenridge. She said that Sunday was for her the most difficult day of the week. Then she smiled and said, 'But how small is my cross compared with what others have to carry.' Patty was too eager for your success and happiness to

Lyda Bevan was popular with the engineering staff.

let it be a trial. I believe she got more thrill out of your accomplishments than you did!"

These precious words from Lyda Bevan only serve to clinch my conviction that the "fifty-fifty" terms of the California Community Property Law only mildly express the debt that a man owes to his wife for his success.

As soon as we were installed in our house, Charlie Bevan gratefully boarded with us for the first six weeks while his cottage was in course of construction next to ours. At last, Charlie's house was finished and he took leave of Breckenridge for a honeymoon measured by hours instead of days. He brought his bride back to our house for a homecoming breakfast to meet Mr. and Mrs. Brooks and the engineering staff, twelve of us in all.

Lyda Bevan was a tremendous asset to our little community. She was especially welcome to Patty because she knew Southern ways and people and was the opposite of hostile to Yankees. She and Patty seemed to understand each other immediately. After boarding with us for two days, the Bevans became our very cordial next door neighbors and fellow officers in the infantry to carry on the Battle of Breckenridge to its final sultry conclusion at the end of the following summer.

The beginning of the end came over the horizon when Harry J. Bauer, Chief Counsel for the Southern California Edison Company, arrived for a three day visit on June 20th. Harry told me that he had made a deal to buy out Walter Wallace and form a new company to be called the Pacific Gasoline Company. I was to wind up my responsibilities as soon as possible and return to California to be Assistant General Manager of the new company. Harry was to be President and General Manager; Alan Morphy was coming over from the Edison Company to be Secretary-Treasurer.

That is how it came about that Patty and I boarded the Texas Pacific train at Cisco, Texas, on Saturday, July 23rd, bound for California and a new and very much more promising enterprise.

Chapter 8

FROM OIL FIELDS TO OFFICE

Patty and I stepped out of the smoky vastness of the old Arcade Station at Los Angeles into the welcome mildness of California's summer evening on Tuesday, July 26th, 1921. I was rather surprised to find Stewart Laughlin, the Company's genial Purchasing Agent, there to meet us. My surprise expanded into ill-concealed glee when, after exchanging greetings, Laughlin led us out to the parking lot and proudly introduced us to our new "company car". It was a robin's-egg blue Marmon sports phaeton. This was prophetic introduction to a new role as executive officer which would test the stamina generated at Breckenridge in an operation twenty times as large.

And so, our eyes were a bit starry as we glided along that summer evening towards brand new worlds to conquer.

For the first few months we made our home with Walter Wallace although he stepped out of office into the status of bond-holder in August.

Then the new management took over and Harry Bauer, Alan Morphy, and I became the "Management Committee". We met every morning in Harry's office to decide what Pacific Gasoline Company would do on that particular day. Harry's secretary was there to record events.

We three ran the business. We had a Board of Directors but they were quite content with the management which soon began to manifest its doings in dividends and rosy reports.

One decision made early in the career of the Management Committee was perhaps the most important and far-reaching in the history of our success. It was a combination of bonus and stock-purchase agreement which invited every employee to share substantially in the profits of the business. Its benefits were so outstanding and so obvious that almost every employee hastened to join the gang and soon became production and profit conscious to a degree that astonished all of us.

It was so successful that, for a long time after we sold out, the doings of Pacific Gasoline Company were legendary lore in the history of the industry in California. At first glance it might seem to be giving away too big a share of the benefit of on-site management and "going-concern" entree for favorable contracts. We did, indeed give away a big share of these benefits. But, to be cold blooded about it, which we were not, we bought with that big share a loyalty which, with all the good will in the world, could not have been obtained in any other way. It was more than loyalty; it was the pride and satisfaction of true proprietorship.

Of course, no amount of employee cooperation could have remedied a failing industrial setting, but ours was just the opposite. The years 1915 to 1926 marked the initial surge of one of the greatest industries in the history of the world — the mass-production of automobiles in the United States. This created a mass demand for motor fuel. Furthermore, refinements in engine design began to put a premium on so-called "high-octane" fuel. Our product furnished precisely the high-octane ingredient. Our raw material was the natural gas produced with the ever-multiplying production of crude petroleum. It was our job to provide the engineering know-how and an eager-beaver personnel to make it effective. The combination made pyramiding profit inevitable.

The bonus auxiliary of the stock ownership plan was tiny in dollar comparison, but it contributed in other ways that made it almost more valuable in promoting loyalty and success. A considerable fillip was also given to the bonus by adding a special premium to all bonus payments at the plant which was judged to have the best operating record for the month.

The "Premium Plant" was determined each month as a result of plant inspection trips made by Harry Bauer and myself. It took about three days each month to visit all twenty-eight plants, but it, too, paid big returns. We knew every employee by

Headquarters at Taft; three plants in 1915, twenty-eight in 1926.

his first-name and usually a good deal about his family. We were able to settle "gripes" almost before they hatched and the plants fairly beamed with neatness and, incidentally, safety.

The fantastic results of all this came to a show-down when, in 1926, the Standard Oil Company of California purchased all of the oil-producing facilities of the Southern Pacific Railroad while our main contract had an unexpired nine years to run. Standard thus became our lessors on all the odd-numbered sections and our competitors on a considerable portion of the even numbered sections throughout the field.

Since our plant capacity exceeded Standard's by a wide margin, it appeared logical to add their gas to ours and let us worry about production. But that was not the policy of Standard of California. Instead they offered to buy us out at a price based on our estimated profit over the next five years. This added up to almost exactly twenty million dollars. Since this would yield between ten and twenty dollars for every shareholder's dollar invested, it would have been fool-hardy to turn it down — and turn it down we did NOT!

During the eleven years following my start on June 1st, 1915, the project had increased from three plants and thirty employees to twenty-eight plants and five hundred employees. During the last five years of this time, about forty-five per cent of the ownership of the company was in the form of stock purchase agreements in the hands of the employees which, if paid in full would have represented an investment of approximately $1,200,-000. But when the company was sold only about half of this total had been paid in. As a result, the five hundred employees who had subscribed, had paid in about $600,000. They received from the proceeds of the sale about nine million dollars cash. Am I justified in calling it "the satisfaction of proprietorship?"

My own original $5,000 invested in Sixteen Oil Company stock had been supplemented by two additional purchases making a total investment of about $50,000. When "pay-day" came on June 24th, 1926, I deposited three checks in the bank which brought my account to a net credit of just over one million dollars. If you don't think that was a thrill, try it some time!

But all this fabulous business experience was accompanied by a family life of Patty and Ken which is quite as thrilling to remember and which must be told before we start drawing checks on that million dollar bank account.

As we began life in these new urban surroundings we felt like old married folks. We knew each others quirks and foibles as well as points of strength. But almost unknown to us was this new phase of our existence. In some respects it was like starting married life all over again. Our whole milieu was completely changed and with it the day-by-day goings-on of husband and wife. Oil field life in the desert is one thing; city life in metropolitan Los Angeles, something very different. For one thing, we had lived and worked almost within constant sight of each other for the

As we began life in these new surroundings, we felt like old married folks.

first six years. Now, like most office workers, I was out of sight at the office or in the field a good part of the time.

It was really a full-time job getting oriented in these new surroundings My new job required every waking moment of my time. And before I was half "in the groove", came the first big test of our employee-management good will program — an oil workers strike.

It was really grim business. The strike was scheduled to begin with the afternoon shift on Monday, September 12th, 1921. I left Los Angeles early on Monday morning and drove to Taft. Already there were little guerilla groups of armed men stopping every car headed for the oil fields to inspect them for passengers who might be "scab" laborers. Having no passengers, I was not turned back, so I was able to reach Taft a couple of hours ahead of the scheduled shut-down. This gave me time to make the rounds of the plants with our slight but stalwart Field Superintendent. The men on the day shift reported that only six of our employees had joined the union and only two of them were on the operating staff.

The "zero-hour" came at 3:00 p.m. A full crew turned out for the afternoon shift. Every plant chugged on, perhaps not quite as merrily as usual, but still they chugged while Beckley and I continued to circulate. It was eerie business on that first night! A shut-down of our plants would have brought matters to a head very promptly because we boosted most of the gas feeding the main supply line to the City of Los Angeles. In fact, the success of the strike of this newly organized Oil Workers Union could hinge on closing down our operations. Rumor had it that Pacific Gasoline Company plants would shut down or would BE shut down. So, as far as we knew that first night, it was "shut down, or else"! Furthermore, the "or else" in a natural gasoline plant or a nitro-glycerin factory could be very unpleasant to think about.

The night wore on, however, and the "grave-yard" shift was on hand full strength when Beckley and I made our third round of the plants about midnight. The relief expressed on the faces of the men when we stepped out from behind our headlights at each plant, would have been laughable if it had not been so deadly serious. Fortunately, however, there were no attempts at sabotage and after the first few days, business went on almost as usual. I was able to return to Los Angeles after twelve days and the strike was soon called off much to the relief of all of us.

Strike tension being over, Patty and I began to look for a place to live. I had to make a trip to the Wallace and Brooks plant at Breckenridge and, as Patty was taking me to the train to see me off, I made a casual remark that was more important than I realized at the time.

And this is what I said: "You know, Patty, when I was a kid in Pasadena we used to gather holly at Christmas time over in the hills west of the Arroyo Seco. I think it is still the most countrified area close to the center of Los Angeles. Why don't

As we climbed out of the car and stood at the top of the bank my emotions were decidedly mixed.

you go over and look around on South San Rafael Avenue and see what you can find?"

When I returned from Texas, I could tell by the glint in Patty's eye that something was beginning to "gel". She said that she had found a lot that she wanted me to see but when I asked her for the details she said: "I don't want to say anything about it till you see it."

I knew from that that there must be a catch to it, but even then, I was hardly prepared for what met my eye on the following day when Patty guided me down San Rafael Avenue. We stopped at a point opposite the old Jevne mansion but Patty was not looking in that direction. Instead, her eyes turned toward the other side of the road to the west. As I followed her eye, all I could see was a rather brief and barren continuation of the dirt roadway of San Rafael Avenue — and beyond that — nothing! It was "nothing" because the terrain dropped away at the property line into the depths of a little ravine that was a tributary of the Arroyo Seco which separated us from the rest of Pasadena.

As we climbed out of the car and stood at the top of the bank, my emotions were decidedly mixed! This property which Patty had discovered was infinitely fascinating in its possibilities, but utterly naked in its present primeval state. It was, indeed, a little gem of a ravine lying within the acute angle formed by the intersection of San Rafael Avenue and Hillside Terrace. Its depth below the street level ranged from sixty feet at the base to perhaps ten feet at the apex. The sides and bottom were covered with shoulder-high dried up mustard stalks. The only saving feature was the presence of two fair-sized and well shaped live-oak trees on the San Rafael side of the ravine. There were also some smaller live-oaks screening the lower end of the ravine.

A little green clump of willows about half way down the otherwise dry bottom caught my eye and we both slithered down the bank toward them. Believe it or not! There was a tiny streamlet of *running* water. To be sure, the output of this little spring could be stored by a child plying a teaspoon, but anyone who has lived in Southern California knows that any water at all, coming out of the ground in late November, is an unheard-of luxury.

I whispered to Patty, "What is the asking price?"

She replied: "It belongs to the Campbell-Johnson Ranch. They frankly admit that they want to sell it because there will soon be an assessment for paving and curbing San Rafael Avenue. They will sell the three acres for three thousand dollars.

I added, "and about fifty thousand more to develop it."

Patty smiled, looked me in the eye and said: "Maybe more!"

With that, we gave each other a big hug and the deal was closed as far as we were concerned. I hastened to make a down payment for the property and the deal *was* closed.

So, there lay our dream home "in the rough" to be sure. I shudder to think of the immensity of the project, but to a husband and wife in their twenties who had just come home after six years in the barren desert, it was the dream of a lifetime. We could talk of nothing else and all sorts of plans began to emerge.

Then, suddenly, tragedy shut out all other thoughts. A telephone call from Beckley at Taft reported that a flash fire at the Lakeview Plant had injured three men, one of them Patty's brother Joseph Pfitzer. I immediately telephoned to the family at Berkeley and Patty's mother and father started south, driving all night, to meet us at Joe's bedside.

Poor Joe was in much worse shape than the other two men. The little hospital at Taft fought a losing battle for his life which ended twelve days later, two days after a far-from-merry Christmas for the four of us.

That event marked the beginning of the tremendous apostleship of Patty's courageous perseverance in her Catholic Faith. Patty's father suddenly realized the tragedy of his former neglect of his religion. He realized, too, that Patty had made it the treasure of her life single-handed, without any help from him. It took this tragedy and Patty's example in meeting it, to start a chain of events that will mingle intimately with all the rest of my life-story.

The first of these events, indeed, did much to sooth for Patty the grief of her loss. The day after the funeral in Berkeley, Mother and Dad went to see a priest and had their marriage rectified. This, too, meant even greater change of heart for Mother. She had grown to womanhood in a family very much prejudiced against the Catholic Church. Now, disregarding that former hostility, her intense loyalty to her husband and her daughter brought it about that she and Dad began to go to Mass together every Sunday without fail.

No wonder the stranger said, "I'll say y' got faith."

And so, cheered by this hopeful outcome, it was not long until Patty and I were again immersed in "Project San Rafael". The contour of our ravine was an ideal setting for an English type of rock-garden. That made English architecture more appropriate than the ubiquitous Spanish design so common in Southern California. So we consulted our friend John Byers for suggestions as to a "wee gate-lodge" that we could perch at the head of our ravine at the very apex of the triangle.

John's design was fabulous. He proposed an inexpensive little English cottage on four levels, starting with a garage and laundry ten feet below street level. We started building in mid-August, 1922, and took keen delight in the time stolen from my job to make visits to our future home.

Twenty years and eighty-five thousand hours of labor later.

My first major project was the installation of a water system on the place. This involved my pipe-fitting experience from the oil field days and, perhaps a tiny tincture of what I am still accused of — super-perfectionism. To crown the project, I installed a pipe-fence down the Hillside Terrace side of the property. I equipped it with sprinkler tips and a water-motor to oscillate its five-hundred-foot length so as to water the entire area from the curb to the bottom of the ravine. I then sowed wild-flower seeds and planted dozens of acorns from our own live-oak harvest.

This done, Patty and I were down by the little spring one Saturday afternoon planning further strategy, when we saw a stranger leaning against the lower rail of the fence and making a general survey of the property. As we looked up, he regarded us with friendly interest and volunteered a comment which became a byword in our family from that day forward. Rather sympathetically he shouted, "I'll say y' got faith!" I will have to admit that, except for the long sprinkler fence and the wildflowers responding to its ministrations, the property did look much more like wilderness than like West-Side Pasadena.

Just for fun, I have figured that some eighty-five thousand man-and-woman hours of labor went into that ravine during the next twenty years. I saw the placing of some seven-hundred tons of beautiful Santa Susana sandstone to form a terraced rock-garden. It also involved the building of four water pools, the largest a forty-by-sixty-foot little lake at the lowest point of the ravine.

All this, not to mention the building of two houses, was to be a big-time job for the rest of our lives together. But in the fall of 1922, the visiting stranger did, indeed, do justice to this vision with his jibe.

Business took me to Washington, D. C. in October, Patty went along for company. That gave us a visit with Father Graham Reynolds. He was teaching Classic and Semitic languages at the Catholic University of America where he had been loaned by Archbishop Cantwell of Los Angeles. It seemed very strange to see Graham in this completely Catholic setting — and stranger still that he seemed quite at home in it.

My business concluded, we went to New York City for a little spree before returning to see to the completion of our new home. My Guest-Book proudly records as of January 23rd, 1923: "Spent the night in our new home at 885 South San

Rafael Avenue, Pasadena." The next morning, one look down our precious ravine, which was already shaping into a garden, left no doubt in our minds that 885 South San Rafael Avenue was to be our home for life!

Mine was a twenty-four-hour-a-day job. There was a constant responsibility for the safe day-and-night operation of all that widely spread array of machinery and the personnel to keep it going. Our lives, however, were crammed with all sorts of precious activities which were no less precious because of the constant alert demanded by the needs of all those moving machines.

Most treasured of these activities were those shared with the friends of our new surroundings. Our dear and life-time friends who came to live in Pasadena about this time were the genial pediatrician, Dr. James E. Harvey, and his wife Loretta Ross Harvey. Jim and I were fourteeners at California and Loretta and Patty were fifteeners.

Another bond between us was a religious one. Loretta and Patty were exceptionally faithful Catholics, while Jim and I were exceptionally cantankerous non-Catholics. I must add, however, that while we both had deep-seated and totally unfounded hereditary prejudices against the Catholic Church which must have been trying to our wives, our hostility never did take the form of meaness or obstruction. I zealously practiced my Episcopalian Faith; Jim zealously practiced Pediatrics which usually occupied him on Sunday mornings.

Another activity which occupied me during these years of business stress was a great variety of hunting. Duck, quail, dove, and deer hunting were all available while we lived at Taft. The same old haunts could be coupled with plant inspection visits even now. But in September, 1924, Harry Bauer, Stuart O'Melveny and I planned our first of several hunting trips into the wonderful high-altitude forests of Arizona.

The State's name, "Arizona" suggests dry desert. It was therefore, a surprise to learn that Arizona has the largest area of national forest land of any state in the Union. It was a hunter's paradise with plenty of wild turkey, bear, and deer — plus the thrill of hunting mountain lions with dogs.

On this first trip we made a fortuitous contact with the Pyle family of hunting guides. They lived near Payson, Arizona at the foot of the great uplift that has hoisted the Mogollon Mesa to an altitude above seven thousand feet.

On this first trip we were treated as tenderfoots and were spoon-fed with easy hunting. It would be different in later years when we were better acquainted.

Even treeing our first lion happened so quickly that he is remembered chiefly because of the preposterous pictures I was able to take on the morning after the hunt. The carcass was frozen so stiff that we were able to stand him upon his four legs and photograph him with the dogs and each member of the party. Harry donned chaps and mounted the beast and I labeled the picture, "Harry the Lyin' Tamer".

On the second day I got a limit of wild turkey, thanks to the art of Louie Pyle. He spotted a little flock in the midst of a meadow and sent me crawling up the stream-bed till I could fire both barrels of my shotgun and put them on the wing. They thundered out with a roar of wings that was like a flock of huge quail. As they sailed over the tree-tops at the upper end of the meadow, Louie came leisurely toward me. We walked together about a hundred yards into the edge of the woods. Then we sat down with our backs against the trunk of a huge Western Yellow Pine. Louie now took out of his pocket a piece of turkey wing-bone about four inches long and a little thinner than a pencil. Putting it in his mouth and cupping his hands over the end, he produced a pensive wail precisely like the questioning call of a barnyard turkey at feeding time. At the second call a young turkey came out from a small bush about fifty yards away and headed straight for us. I was almost ashamed to shoot it, but after all, that was what had brought us here. So, I pulled the trigger once, and, at Louie's signal did *not* go to retrieve the bird.

Harry Bauer "The Lyin' Tamer."

Louie Pyle guides me home with a five point buck.

Louie again began his tune on the wing-bone and this time, believe it or not, a young bird flew into a high perch in the very tree we were sitting under. So, after about ten minutes of musical comedy on Louie's part, I had my limit of turkey for the season.

Our deer-hunt the next day is memorable because of our late return on foot with a five-point buck loaded on Louie's tired horse. We were perhaps twelve miles from camp when the sun set and darkness seemed to gather very fast. There were endless gullies and knolls and meadows and streamlets to cross. They all looked alike to me. I could not make out a single guiding landmark. Soon real night reached its normal stride and the terrain receded into vague shadows and the ground under our feet seemed to vanish two or three steps ahead of us. But still Louie kept plodding on, pausing only now and then to look up through the trees at the starry sky. Sometimes he seemed to sniff the air as if to share in the horse's keen sense of smell.

Finally, our steps seemed to encounter many small chunks of broken rock and Louie stopped as if puzzled. Then, to my surprise, he struck a match and examined one of these small stones as if expecting to find a direction written on it. And, as if he had done just that, he said: "Well, we're nearer camp than I thought." He then turned to the right up a long easy slope and, upon reaching the gentle leveling off at the crest, we could see our campfire less than half a mile away.

It is strange how that picture of Louie crouching to examine the color of the ground by match-light was to fix itself in my memory. It has become a sort of symbol of guidance to rightness. Louie was truly a competent guide provided by God for my safety. A less competent guide could easily have led me on another quarter mile in the direction we were headed and pitched us both over the thousand-foot precipice of the Mogollon Rim. Thanks to Louie, this trip ended safely and with many happy memories.

There were many other interesting events sandwiched into these last years of my business life. They were all threads in the tapestry which God was shaping for my life when that final payday from the Standard of California was to give me a better chance to think about Him.

My final assurance of that pay-day came late in May, 1926. It was still cool enough for Patty and me to be sitting in the dark before the open fire in our little living room. The telephone rang and, coming back after answering it, I took Patty in my arms and said: "That was Harry Bauer calling from San Francisco. The deal is closed and Standard of Cal takes over next month. Will you sell for a million?"

Patty's answer was, "Whatever you say!"

And so it came about that, at age thirty-four, I left my last job and entered sixteen years of what is sometimes called "retirement". For me, it was the most active period of my life. But, as God intended, it brought me face to face in the prime of life with that great secret question: "How come, myself and my doings in this world?" If this had not happened to me, I would probably still be hacking away at the material side of life without time to think of my reason for being here.

Chapter 9

THE BUSINESS OF LEISURE

The farewell meeting of the Pacific Gasoline Company was a really joyous affair for all those present. It was a barbecue picnic with "Bill" and Harry Bauer at their Sawmill Mountain Ranch on Sunday, June 26th, 1926. Almost everybody except the men actually on "tour" was present. And enjoy it they did, as can be imagined, since almost everyone present was a beneficiary of the twenty-million-dollar-pay-off of the previous week.

Late that afternoon Patty and I took leave of Pacific Gasoline Company and turned with enthusiasm to "The Business of Leisure" which was to occupy us for the next sixteen years.

An obvious first of this business was the investment of our new capital fund. I was quite amazed at the amount of advice offered on that score. Most of it involved fabulous ways of doubling my investment and, incidentally, plunging back into speculative business activities. I had more of this world's goods than I had ever dreamed of owning. Was there any real reason why I should carry on in business? Was it unethical to step out when my services could be useful to others? Certainly, if an emergency needed my services. That did happen in World War Two and I answered it. But to stay on now seemed more likely to be depriving some better man of my job.

Managing my own investments could be a full time job but I had no more desire to be my own investment counselor than to be my own doctor or lawyer. So, I turned my investment job over to my friend Arthur Clifford and never regretted that decision. When things went wrong in the nineteen-thirties I always took it as his worry and not mine.

As a matter of fact, I never did consider myself retired from business. I continued to share an office with Alan Morphy in Los Angeles. My time gradually became more fully occupied than ever before. And that continued until I offered my services to the Petroleum Administration for War in 1942.

I can now see the gentle hand of Divine Providence "reaching from end to end mightily, and ordering all things sweetly." My life has been crammed throughout with tiny unnoticed beginnings. They have been like the guided flight of missiles, sure but unseen. They have brought about momentous results. They have led me ever so gently to an appreciation of the love of God which is so obvious in restrospect and so hidden when it is happening. There is no other phrase so aptly describing God's part as: "ordering all things sweetly". And yet, I have often tried His patience by my cantankerous self-will.

I used to think, sometimes, of that long night spent in the bus stalled in a blizzard up-grade from Bailey's Ranch in the Antelope Valley, a long ten years earlier. But how much did I remember of the promise I made to God that night? I fear it was set aside in favor of star-boat racing at Balboa, fishing trips with the Bauers, and entertaining many welcome guests of our own. One of those guests was my dear brother Father Graham, home for the summer from the Catholic University of America. That brief visit did much to restore our old brother-to-brother camaraderie. That, too, gave me access to another source of grace.

It was during that visit that Graham was inspired to make a fantastic prophecy. I was out on the beach in front of the house working on the star-boat ways. Graham, watching me through the window, remarked to Patty: "Kenny always does everything with all his might, doesn't he? Some day he'll be a Catholic and when he falls he'll fall hard."

If he had said that to me, I would have called it preposterous nonsense. Dear God, you must have chuckled a little at the accuracy of that "preposterous nonsense".

Returning from Balboa in September, we stepped into a new project. Our wee-gate-lodge definitely needed a maid's room, a guest room, and an adequate kitchen and dining room. John Byers was again consulted and again furnished just the answer. But, alas, when work was begun it became obvious that our little

Our Wee-gate-lodge definitely needed to be enlarged.

Loading up at Kencott for Balboa Beach.

gate-lodge was in no condition to be the nucleus of the house of our plans. Termites had already begun to work on the foundation timbers. A very brief inspection made it clear that only one answer was available — start again from the grass-roots! So, the contractor's crew became a demolition squad instead of house builders.

We salvaged and stored the beautiful oak plank flooring from the living room as a souvenir of our happy four years of occupancy. Then we sold the rest of the salvage for a price that left a balance of thirty-five dollars above the cost of demolition. So — the picture was considerably changed for us!

Again, God must have chuckled as my thoughts began to advert to a conversation I had a few days earlier with a friend who had just returned from a trip around the world on one of the Dollar Liners. At the time, I had thought — No, we will be too busy with house-building. Now, God whispered: "So what?"

And that is how it came about that, when Patty and I applied for a United States Passport a few days later, we were puzzled as to what to fill in on the dotted line after the caption: Bearers address in the United States. I gave the law offices of Bauer Wright and MacDonald as our address.

Two weeks later, Patty and I boarded the "Padre" at Glendale. We had just had dinner with the Harveys and were escorted by the Bauers and Betty Reynolds. We were bound for Berkeley and then the orient.

On Wednesday, January 19th, 1927, we sailed out through the Golden Gate on the old Matson liner "Matsonia", bound for Honolulu and beyond. Of course, there was a thrill of joy in all this. I will have to admit, however, that there were mixed emotions as we watched our home-land and North America fade into nothingness behind those inscrutable motionless gulls coasting along powered by the ship's air wave.

Our spirits were soon refreshed by the happy new experience of life aboard ship. Officers, crew, and passengers now constituted "the people of the world" and a fraternal bond prevailed. Our initiation to this new status of the sea seemed only beginning when Patty's cousin, Leslie McCabe came aboard at Honolulu with beautiful floral leis and took us to the old Moana Hotel. We jilted the Moana a few days later to go to the newly opened Royal Hawaiian.

Les McCabe loaned us his car and this immensely increased our enjoyment of our week-long stay on the Island of Oahu.

On the excursion to the Volcano Island of Hawaii we enjoyed the beautiful fern forests and the wierd lava-tubes. But *the* event of the day was a chance to watch a husky golfer drive a hole-in-one into the crater of the Kilauea Volcano. It was a beautiful three-hundred-yard drive, but in that three-thousand-yard cup it made man seem very tiny.

Returning to Honolulu, we boarded the President Wilson on February 5th. There we found ourselves assigned to a very comfortable stateroom which was to be our "home" for the next fifty-two days. The first leg was the thirteen-day journey between Honolulu and Kobe, Japan. It was made memorable by the experience of a real storm at sea.

On the third day out the sea became unbelievably rough. Having had no previous experience for comparison, we did not know how scared to be. The officers were not too convincing in the tone of voice with which they assured us that all was well. Their tone was still less convincing when the ship shuddered up from the depths of a trough with hundreds of tons of green water pouring over the bow and down the scuppers on either side. They admitted, moreover, that the wind had reached a velocity of eighty miles per hour.

Our stay at Kobe and the excursion from there to Kyoto, as at every other stop we made, was punctuated with all sorts of purchases of things useful or not-so-useful. One event not involving a purchase occurred on the main shopping street of Kyoto. There, in the teeming hubbub of the street was a flattish heap of rags — No! I saw it move — then I came nearer. Could that be a human being with a soul and what had been a body? Yes, it was — a leper.

Many years later, I was reading the life story of St. Teresa of Avila. She describes what God permitted her to see when a priest, sunk deep in mortal sin, stood before her to place the Body of Christ on her tongue in Holy Communion. Her description made the thought of that leper flash into my mind. St. Teresa brought that priest back to repentance by telling him what she had seen. The combination has given me a healthy dread of sin!

Leaving Japan, our first stop in the mainland of Asia was at Shanghai. It was memorable because of the genial hospitality of Julean Arnold, Commercial Attache of the American Consulate, and his wife who, as Gertrude Davis, was a friend of my childhood days in Pasadena.

The highlight of the visit was a twenty-one-course Chinese dinner served in a private room in a Chinese restaurant on the evening of our departure. Everything was delicious and beautifully served in portions ample for about six people. The host could bring as many as he chose. If any portions were left over, they might be put in a basket and taken home. That residue, we were told, is what Chinese mean by the word "Chop Suey".

After the dinner, the party adjourned to an entertainment at the Plaza Hotel; then we were taken to the eleven o'clock tender back to the President Wilson.

Our stateroom was a welter of shopping loot. Two of the items stand out in my memory — especially as to price. One was a carton containing twelve quarts of assorted Scotch, Bourbon, cognac and rum; total price $13.50. The other was a box containing three hand-tailored Palm Beach suits; total price $37.50! Such was life before inflation took over.

There was a dismal cold fog and rain as we pulled out into the East China Sea headed for Hong Kong. It was certainly no kind of weather to be out of sight of land in a small Chinese fishing junk, even a beamy one. I was quite unprepared, however, for the proof of that fact which came our way.

A considerable shouting in Chinese dialect from members of our crew drew me to the rail as our ship slowed down almost to a stop. There, clinging to the skeg of a completely overturned junk, was a pitiful lone Chinese coolie drenched in the icy water and shouting for help. He was the sole survivor of a crew of four carried out to sea in the storm.

While our great ship was standing by doing nothing, waves were occasionally washing over the poor shivering victim on the wrecked junk. Finally, a wave tore loose his clutching hold on the skeg. He was carried off and disappeared beneath the surface. As the ship's engines began to throb and we pulled past the junk, his body was just visible sinking into the depths. The conversation was very subdued at the midday meal that day.

Our Hong Kong visit was brief and I guess a little too strenuous because we both took to our beds with flu. We were only partly ambulatory when Patty's sorority sister, Blanche Casey, came aboard at Manila. Her friendly ministrations helped to revive us but we were glad to take to bed again and grateful for warmer weather as we headed for Singapore.

My memory of Singapore and the side trip to Jahore is an amazing polyglot of voices, races, colors, and dress. One priceless little item of it I caught with my movie camera — an aged Maylayan man with a youngster strapped to a basket seat on his back. He was utterly oblivious of the fact that he was being photographed. The result was about the best fifty feet out of three thousand odd that recorded our trip.

Except for one glorious day at Colombo, the next three weeks were filled with the joys of a sea voyage. As we crossed the Indian Ocean everything conspired for camaraderie, relaxation and sport. Everyone entered into the enjoyment of it. The final event was a fancy dress ball. Patty's ingenuity won for her the vote of the most beautiful costume. She had put it together out of fabrics purchased en route. We debarked at Suez and so ended our fifty-two-day voyage on the President Wilson. There, a new and very different "voyage" began.

Our stay in Egypt lasted nine days. It yielded many new experiences, some precious, some not-so-precious. A sight worth the whole trip, though, was the solid gold beautifully engraved mummy-case which had enclosed the body of King Tutankhamen. This was exhibited at the Cairo museum together with many other precious objects taken from the king's tomb.

On April 2nd we reached Luxor, an intensely interesting land of antiquity some five-hundred miles deeper in Africa up the Nile from Cairo. The dragoman assigned to us for the morning tour was extra-attentive in guiding us to King Tut's tomb in the Valley of Kings and the Rameses Temple. His reason soon became apparent. He proposed a very "special" tour for the afternoon which he himself would organize.

I should have known better, but he made it sound so interesting that we agreed to go. After lunch he called for us in a very dilapidated topless Model T Ford and off we went, Patty and I in the back seat; our guide and his "helper" in front. It was indeed an interesting glimpse into the ordinary goings-on in the farming country of interior Egypt.

On the return trip, however, while still about five miles outside of Luxor, the driver suddenly slowed down, turned into an alleyway between high mud walls, stopped at the mud-walled end, and shut off his motor. I may have been in more helpless danger at other times, but never before had it been quite so obvious. Here I sat, armed only with my Singapore Malacca cane, prized for its pithy weightlessness. Our two husky "guardians" put their heads together in mumbled consultation. I did have sense enough to remain perfectly quiet. After what seemed like an age, perhaps three minutes, without a word or glance at me, our guide started the motor, backed out of the hide-out and headed for Luxor. I never had a clue as to what strategem was used by Divine Providence to change the plans of those two husky bandits. Its effect on me has been lifelong assurance that God is in complete command of *everything* that happens.

Perhaps they only staged the performance so that I would say nothing when they charged me double the price of the Cook's tour of that morning, At any rate, Patty and I exchanged meaningful looks a couple of days later when the Cairo newspaper headlined the murder, near Alexandria, of an American husband and wife for the man's pocket money.

We left Cairo by train for Jerusalem. The hostile desert that we could see as we sat comfortably looking out of the train window, recalled the flight into Egypt of Mary, Joseph, and the Child Jesus. They went on foot over almost two hundred miles of waterless desert through country that no one would ordinarily have attempted except in an armed caravan. At their destination the people would be strangers, hostile to the Jews and ignorant of their language. They were to stay for an unknown length of time with no passport except a dream vision reported to Mary by Joseph. Except for Joseph's word, the Child's life would appear to be far safer in Bethlehem! But they left — at midnight — for Egypt. That makes Mary my exemplar of courage derived from utter trust in God!

Next day, our arrival in Jerusalem brought amazement and distress to my Protestant eyes. Hostility between the Arabs and the Jews and the many different kinds of Christians was obvious wherever one turned. I was told that the keys of the Church of the Holy Sepulcher were in the hands of the Turks because nobody else could be trusted with them. That may or may not have been true, but the atmosphere of it was everywhere. Where the Prince of Peace had been, the Principalities of Darkness seemed now to hold the place under a curse.

I was much happier while spending hours sitting on a little second-floor balcony at the Grand Hotel about one hundred yards from the Jaffa Gate. The ever-changing variety of comers and goers was beyond imagining.

We did much sight-seeing in and around Jerusalem. It was intensely interesting but my Protestant being was repelled by it. I for one, was glad to take the train for Alexandria and to board the President Van Buren bound for Naples.

Our visit to the Holy Land had left me with a vague sense of shame that often came back to me and made me thoughtful. The obvious disunity among those who considered themselves Christians seemed to cast a blight on the whole mission of Christ to the human race. Since He was God, how could there be more than one interpretation of His will?

On the Van Buren we were happy to resume thoughts about the real quest of this journey of ours. Much of our "spare" time on shipboard had been spent sitting in our deck chairs planning our new home. I had brought along a little drawing kit and by the time we reached Naples we had a good many sheets loaded with plans. It was to be an English house built of stone with half-timbered gables and a shingle tile roof. Our delight was to fit it to the terrain upon which it was to be built. The real business of gathering details would have to wait until we reached British territory. It had already become a quest, however, by the time we reached Naples on the cold and windy afternoon of Holy Saturday, April 16th, 1927.

The immediate business in hand was Easter Sunday in Naples. It was our first experience in a really Catholic environment. Patty, of course, found it a godsend to be back once more where the fulfillment of her religious duties would not require contriving to avoid impatience on my part. She was, naturally, especially grateful to have this come about on the eve of Easter Sunday.

To me, it was a bit of an eye-opener to observe the take-it-for-granted devotion of so many people everywhere. One thing that impressed us both was the informality with which religious devotion seemed to be linked with everyday life.

The eighteen days spent in Italy left many cherished memories. The beauty of the country and its seacoast, the countless treasures of art and architecture, all blended with the unity of work and worship. It gave me a sense of admiration and a little questioning wonder.

The transition from Italy to Switzerland was like going into a different world. At Florence it was warm spring and the height of the tourist season. As the train emerged from the twelve-mile-long-Simplon Tunnel and steamed into Brig, Switzerland, it seemed as if, by the waving of a magic wand, the train crew, the language, the money, and the climate, all reappeared in a different form.

From Brig we went to Zermatt at the foot of the Matterhorn on May 5th, the first train of the season. The dazzling light of a crystal-clear day was intensified by reflection from the great snow-clad mountain. Millions of crocus were blooming right up to the edge of the snow blanket.

Two days later we had an even greater thrill going to the top of Jungfrau by a cog-railroad inside the mountain.

Next day we did some shopping in Zurich. One insignificant item recorded in my vest-pocket cash book was: "Bolt of heavy linen sheeting — 84 Fr." It would long since have been forgotten but for its destination which was never dreamed of by either of us when it was purchased. Forty-two years later it reposes on a hanger in the little sacristy of the chapel in the Pfitzer Memorial Tower at Westminster Abbey, British Columbia. It is a priest's alb which I am permitted to keep as a memento. Little did Patty or I know, when she made it thirty years ago, that it would be worn by her husband!

Our next move involved one of the most interesting and beautiful trips of our brief crossing of Europe; an eight-hour voyage down the Rhine from Mainz to Cologne.

The next twelve days were spent in a whirl of shopping and sight-seeing in Paris. We were there on May 21st when Lieutenant Charles Lindbergh completed his nonstop flight from New York. A week later, in London, we were stalled in traffic while on the upper deck of a bus directly in front of the American Embassy. The tie-up was the result of the throng of people struggling to get a glimpse of the now famous flier as he was being ushered into the Embassy. Our position was better than any possible planned reservation. Here we sat on top of a bus, not over thirty feet from the door of the Embassy, and watched the whole much-cheered event.

But, here in London, everything began to center around our twofold quest: first, ideas for an English house, Second, ideas for items to furnish it. The first was immediately fortified by contact with the English Speaking Union. The second was equally aided by Mrs. Fanny Rowan Young who, like Gertrude Arnold at Shanghai, was an old friend of the Reynolds family. Fanny introduced us to a veteran of World War One, Mr. Sydney Williams, whose right leg was absent up to and including the ball joint at the hip. He was the most cheerful cripple I have ever known. And, with a crutch or cane or just hopping around, he was also the most lively.

Where Sydney got his knowledge of and his access to English antiques I do not know, but he certainly had both. He seemed to take delight in ferreting out and finding things to please us rather than to make us pleased with what he happened to have in stock. Everything he sold us was authentic and priced to give value rather than profit.

I know whereof I speak. Upon returning home, I saw it through customs myself. It arrived in a case that looked like a freight car and weighed about a ton. During this transaction I became well acquainted with the head of the U. S. Customs Office in Los Angeles. When it was released, he congratulated me and volunteered the statement that it was the easiest to identify as genuine antiques that he had even seen entered at the Port of Los Angeles!

And now the travel part of our quest was made fascinating by our contact with the English Speaking Union. The genial Secretary had written notes to a number of prominent "County People" who had beautiful homes which she wanted us to see. She gave us an outline of the trip that she thought would be most useful in making these contacts. She also gave us much practical advice.

But, armed with these notes and this advice, I was a bit awed at the prospect of bursting up to a great country estate and volunteering to carry off snapshots of all that took our fancy in their private homes! It is no secret that many of the inhabitants of the British Isles look upon American tourists as boastful, money-oriented, ill mannered specimens of the human race to be treated with rather cold disdain. And I must admit that I have witnessed a few events which would justify such an appraisal.

With all this in mind, we were somewhat apprehensive as we rented a very humble little Morris-Cowley roadster and set out on our quest, armed with a Kodak and a list of names.

Then came the surprise that made the next forty-three days and three thousand miles one of the most enjoyable experiences of our married life. From the very first telephone call to our last farewell at Southampton, the British "county" people most generously reversed whatever might have been our thoughts about their aloofness. They astounded us by their friendly acceptance of this unknown pair of American tourists. The notion that we were interested — not just in houses and gardens — but in getting ideas about our own planned house and garden, was the "Open Sesame" to their hearts and to their homes. They not only made us their guests and friends, but they invited us to take snapshots of their houses, furniture, window hardware, rooflines — anything that interested us. They even called up their neighbors who had never heard of us and made them feel complimented by the fact that they had something special that must be photographed.

Thus, England became for us a land of people and their homes, not just another land for sight-seeing. We did our share of the latter as well. We were within eye-range of most of the "tight little isle" from Cornwall to Inverness.

We returned to London for a final week of shopping and then, with an unbelievable amount of loot and precious ammunition for our house plans, we sailed from Southampton on the Canadian Pacific Steamer Montroyal in mid-July. We reached Quebec after seven days having been slowed down by two days of fog and a copious sprinkling of icebergs.

Next day, we started our five-day train trip across Canada punctuated by its marvelous scenery and climaxed by a day at Lake Louise. I decided that God must have made the setting of Lake Louise in competition with Himself as the ultimate in grandeur.

The final joy of homecoming was not the least bit dimmed by the fact that we had no home to go to. In fact, it was heightened by the glee of comparing our plans with the actual site. It was a comfort to climb into our own car once more when the "Padre" stopped at Glendale, California, on Sunday, July 31st. After Mass at St. Andrew's Church in Pasadena and dinner at the Annandale Golf Club, we hastened on down to Balboa Beach to spend two happy days with Bill and Harry Bauer before moving into our own rented house two doors up the Bay Front.

Chapter 10

MANY THREADS

The joy of our stay at Balboa Beach during that August of 1927 was subject to competition in several other directions. Obviously, we were bursting to get our house-plans and pictures in the hands of an architect. But there was another little project that was destined to occupy us intensively during certain months of the years ahead.

Alexander Macdonald, Harry Bauer's law partner, and Doctor Rea Smith had become avid members of the Flat Rock Club on the North Fork of the Snake River in Idaho where dry-fly fishing for rainbow and native trout is at its best. Before we left for England, Alex and Eileen Macdonald had invited Patty and me to be their guests at this delightful spot as soon as we could get organized after our return from abroad.

And so it was to be expected that this invitation was well remembered when we were shopping near the famous Hardy Brothers tackle shop in London. Once there, we allowed ourselves to be fitted out with everything recommended by the very courteous (and astute) salesman.

And when I say "we" I mean just that! Whether by inspiration, good sense, or just luck, I started a practice in those first purchases which netted tremendous dividends for both of us in the years to come. I never bought myself any fishing equipment that I did not match it with equal equipment for my wife. How many times I have ribbed husbands who wished their wives took an interest in fishing the way mine did. But that came later. At the moment, Patty was only mildly interested in our visits to Hardy Brothers. Nevertheless, she had that priceless quality of compatibility that made her want to like whatever I liked.

And so, in early August we consulted with the Macdonalds and set the date of our departure for August 26th. We also joined with them, sight unseen, in the purchase of a tract of land straddling more than half a mile of the Snake River a couple of miles down-stream from the Flat Rock Club, at the foot of Coffee Pot Rapids.

In spite of our mighty preparations for departure, we managed to make contact with the Pasadena Architect, David Ogilvie. We were delighted with the glee which sparkled in his eye when he scanned our trophies. He was most exultant when I showed him a shingle tile which I had rescued from a damaged pig-sty on the last day of our tour in England. And this brought it about that ours was the first of the many lovely roofs of shingle tile as the sequel to that damaged pig-sty. How tiny are the threads of God's providence!

How little did I suspect the course that these threads were preparing for me! The sly beginning of one of them was another two-day visit from my brother Graham during this hectic interim at Balboa. It gave another close tie that cemented our longer reunion of the previous year.

Graham's priestly life had been a strenuous one. He had spent four years abroad at Oxford and the University of Paris to qualify for professorship at the Catholic University of America. All this had undermined his health in a way that doctors seemed to find difficult to diagnose. So, about the only thing prescribed was to return to California for the summer and take a complete rest. Now, in our living room at Balboa he was once more my four-years-older brother of childhood days. It was a great consolation to each of us during that brief two days that he was our guest.

All too quickly, however, August 26th arrived. We and the Macdonalds, loaded with fishing gear, boarded the train bound for Trude, Idaho. We were met on Sunday morning by Doctor Rea and Molly Smith who took us to the Flat Rock Club for a huge breakfast. Then, I was invited to unlimber my Hardy equipment for a try on that beautiful stretch of dry fly water.

What appealed to me most on that particular day was the perfect adaptability of that water for learning the art. Its easy

Dining room at Kencott.
"It was really a dream come true."

flow of current and uniform gravelly bottom made wading exceptionally easy. The many patches of water plants made good cover for the awkward angler as well as for the abundant population of trout. This combination rewarded my maiden go at dry fly fishing with five perfect specimens, three rainbows and two cut-throats, the smallest just under a pound. The combination clinched my career as a dry-fly purist. I was hooked!

But greater thrills were in store when we all went down river next morning to inspect our new venture which common consent had already named "Coffee Pot Lodge". Our big half-mile of the river gave promise of excellent dry-fly water. The cabin site was on a long reverse curve of the River which gave a fine view of most of our water. All this kept us busy planning the camp and trying out the fishing. It seemed no time till our three weeks were ended and we were boarding the Yellowstone Special for Salt Lake City and home.

The next two months were spent working in our garden or hounding Ogilvie with our house plans. Ogilvie's plans were so pains-taking that he had embodied almost every item found in our snapshots. Peter Hall, the contractor, was equally diligent. The net result was really a work of love that has been cherished and appreciated by every owner in its history.

We moved in on July 6th, 1928. It was really a dream come true. In all the years we lived there, neither of us ever thought of anything we would have changed if we had it to do over again.

And so, our full time job of house-building became a fuller time job of housekeeping and gardening and living. God chose this time to begin to weave more threads into the tapestry which meant more than I realized at the time.

Graham's health had worsened during the previous year at Washington. He was advised to return to California and undertake a thorough physical check-up. When he arrived in Pasadena in mid-June we were surprised to see how well he looked and yet how utterly "tired" he seemed to be. He seemed baffled, too, because tiredness was his only symptom. The diagnostician to whom he went, after lengthy tests and X-rays, was unable to lay hold of any prognosis.

So, he pronounced Graham's trouble "nervous exhaustion" and sent him to a psychiatrist. That gentleman put him to painting all sorts of lurid scenes in oil. Then, after two months with no improvement, he shipped the poor priest off to us at Coffee Pot Lodge. Fortunately we were able to give him a comfortable welcome, although it was no solution.

The next four months must have been a nightmare for poor Graham. He felt utterly ill and yet the doctors, unable to read the symptoms, were skeptical and unsympathetic. The psychiatrist kept insisting that the only hope for full recovery lay in solitude away from any distractions.

By this time, I was really disturbed. I sensed in some degree the disquiet of mind caused by this frustration, and yet, what was to be done? At last, in mid-February, I began to explore the possibilities of giving the psychiatrist's scheme a try.

God seemed to take the matter in hand. He prompted the idea that the back country of San Diego County was well adapted for our scheme, both in climate and in seclusion. Then, He brought success to our first exploratory trip to an agent in Escondido. In answer to my inquiry for a secluded spot for a hermitage, the agent replied: "That's the exact description of what came into my office last week! It's forty acres of rolling hills up in Moose Canyon and there's a cabin and a water well on the property."

With that, he took us up to inspect "Camel Rock Ranch", so named because of the similarity to a kneeling camel displayed by one of several large rock outcroppings. The rest was a riot of budding mountain lilac which God had added to clinch the deal. I took an option and returned later with Graham to get his final verdict.

My heart aches now to recall what must have been his thoughts. The cabin was indeed primitive. The well was a hundred yards from the cabin. As we were returning from an inspection of the well, Graham lagged behind. I was astonished to see that he was having difficulty with the up-hill grade which was so slight that I had not even noticed it.

Things looked rather dim, to say the least. It was obvious that Graham could not cope with the situation as it was.

I said, "Do you think you could handle it if I install a gas-driven pump at the well and put a tank on the porch? I will have a carpenter put the cabin in shape and put a stack of firewood on the porch." That cheered Graham considerably and he said he thought he could handle it all right.

There was a little farm house about a half-mile from the cabin. We were relieved to find it occupied by a good capable family of country people. The husband was quite willing to take the job of fitting the cabin for occupancy and the teenage boy and girl seemed keen to have a neighbor in the cabin.

With that much settled, I went to Escondido and closed the deal and made arrangements to get the project under way. Graham's spirit seemed to rise now that the practicability of the project was really being provided. He was perceptably more at ease during the rest of his stay with us.

Finally the cabin was ready. So, with a trailer-load of gear, we took Graham to Camel Rock Ranch to put all in readiness for his return later to take up residence. The pump was put in action and the water tank on the porch was filled. Graham seemed quite pleased with the whole project and we returned to Pasadena in high spirits.

On Saturday morning I was working at my desk at home when the telephone rang and I answered.

It was Graham's voice responding, "Kenny, I'm going to have to call it off; I don't think I can handle it."

"Graham", I said, "I am the one who has backed you when everyone else has said you would never go." That was true but I had no idea of its impact upon Graham.

"All right", he said, "I'll go; I'll *make* it go!"

I was alarmed at the tone of his voice and said: "I didn't mean that as a challenge."

He replied, "That's all right; with your backing I will go down there and try to make it. Give me a couple of weeks and then we can have a better idea for the future."

After that, Graham set his face to the ordeal and on Tuesday, April 9th, my nephew, Henry Reynolds, collected Graham and his clothes and his food and, after calling at the nearby farm, left Graham a lonely hermit, at the cabin.

Ten days later, Patty and I left with Lawrence and Dorothy vander Leck for a three-day visit at Death Valley. On our return, we stopped, intending to spend the night at the Harvey House at Barstow.

While we were at supper in the Harvey House dining room, I was dumfounded to hear my name paged at the desk. I hastened to report and was directed to the telephone desk. There, I was connected with my brother-in-law Arthur Mace. He told me that Graham had been found dead in his cabin, the morning before, by the farm boy and his sister.

I later learned that these dear young people had immediately become Graham's friends. Graham had made a deal with the boy to tutor him in Latin while the boy would do the chores which Graham was unable to do.

The children, however, were alarmed by Graham's languor and kept a close watch on the cabin. On the morning of Saturday, April 20th, 1929, no smoke was coming from the stovepipe. The children hastened to the cabin to find that he had apparently just finished dressing himself and had fallen back on the bed, instantly dead. The children ran home in frightened haste and telephoned the Coroner and later got word to the family. Then Arthur's intuition had located me at Barstow.

My feelings can only be faintly imagined! In fact, it is hard for me to imagine them myself. It almost seemed as if I had engineered the whole pitiful tragedy. The Coroner's autopsy disclosed that death was the result of aortic stenosis. Doctors have told me that it is inconceivable that such a condition would not have been disclosed by X-ray. It did me little good, however, to recall that my words and acts which had resulted in Graham's death, were prompted by the medical advice that Graham had reported to me. My soul really did suffer anguish.

Patty and I boarded the Santa Fe train at Barstow at two o'clock on Monday morning and arrived in Pasadena at seven. We were met by Arthur Mace and went to Camel Rock with the Maces and my sister Jessie Terrell. We were consoled to learn what the little neighbors had done for Graham during his lonely suffering.

Patty, of course, realized more than any of us the anguish of a priest who is left to die without the support of the Last Sacraments. But the Protestant family had their eyes and ears very much enlightened during the next few days. I for one, was amazed to see and hear the evidence of love and honor that was paid to my brother. An unbelievable number of priests and lay people, all strangers to us, came to pay tribute to Father Graham Reynolds.

Father James P. O'Shea preached a memorial sermon at St. Andrew's Church in Pasadena. It sank deep in my memory. One thought that was utterly new to me was the preciousness of the death of one who had been a faithful servant of God. He would now receive the reward for which his whole life had been dedicated. That sermon also gave me esteem for Father O'Shea which bore fruit three years later.

Next day, we were even more amazed when we all attended the funeral at St. Vibiana Cathedral in Los Angeles. We found ourselves seated near the front surrounded by about fifty priests and as many Sisters. Archbishop Cantwell offered the Mass and another short sermon was crammed with ideas about death, all of which were new to me.

And so another portion of the tapestry of God's design was completed. Many threads were added to this tapestry that stemmed from deeper sources than I knew. God had His reasons for allowing me to feel so keenly my part in this event.

My memory often drifted back over the things that were said and done. It gave me some new ideas about the purpose of life. These ideas were gradually changing my concept of God and His relationship to me.

All this simmered in my mind without being put into words during many months in which I, like Martha of Bethany, was "busy about many things".

First in order of time, came the pay-off of my practice of duplicating for my wife all my purchases of fishing gear for myself. In 1927 and 1928 on the Snake River, both at the Flat Rock Club and at Coffee Pot Lodge, Patty had made a brave effort to learn to cast a dry-fly in a manner appropriate to the quality of her equipment. But let's face it; she just could not learn to coordinate her movements, and that is all that it takes to learn to cast a dry-fly well. She almost gave up a time or two, but rallied whenever one of us brought in a two or three pound rainbow. By the summer of 1929, however, she had at least succeeded in keeping the fly in the air instead of in her hair or on the back of her sweater.

So, there was hopeful promise of success as we left for Coffee Pot Lodge in mid-August. We went that year by way of Oregon for a try at the fishing on the McKenzie River at Thomson's Resort. There, the skillful maneuvering on the part of Dayton Thomson, the boatman, put Patty in reach of two or three fine "red-sides" for which that River is famous. This gave Patty considerable confidence and, when we reached Coffee Pot Lodge ten days later, she was ready for a try that same afternoon.

While I was still unpacking our gear, Patty set out upstream arrayed in everything ever found in a dry-fly catalog and some things beside. Her light-weight balloon-cloth waders were belted just under her armpits. Her olive drab canvas jacket was designed by her husband and was tailor-made with pockets in the elbow-length sleeves and breast, side, and back. Her folding Hardy landing-net and her eight-foot-six-inch: four-and-one-half-ounce Hardy fly-rod made her look invincible to me as she trudged along the trail toward the "Percolator" pool where she had decided to make her first try.

A slight bend in the River concealed the Percolator Pool from my view as I started out after her about fifteen minutes later, bound for the "Sitting Rock Pool" further up the River at the foot of Coffee Pot Rapids. I will never forget what met my eye as I stepped down to the river bank about fifty yards below the Percolator. There wasn't much of her to see because she was out in the very middle of the river with the water about three inches below the top of her waders. But what I did see filled me with unforgettable glee! Arms raised to keep her elbows out of the water, and rod straight up with a perfect stance, she was managing the most acrobatic three-pound rainbow trout I have ever seen. He took line off the reel up-stream three or four times and went high in the air about ten times. But Patty handled her rod like a veteran and gradually eased herself into knee-deep water near the bank keeping just the right tension on the line and finally slipped the net under his tail and turned toward me.

A slight bend in the river concealed the "Percolator Pool."

By that time I was in the water but not near enough to be accused of offering any help whatever, even by word. She had done it all by herself and with consummate skill! The wet embrace that followed and the stars in her eyes told me that the rest of my angling career would be in loving competition with a wife who was an addict and a skillful one at that!

That three-pound rainbow really had a profound influence on the behavior of the Reynolds family during the next twelve years. It ended only when World War Two ended my retirement from business. Patty had formerly twitted me now and then about being a perfectionist in various pursuits, but not any more! In fact, from then on, I had to keep on my toes to be anywhere near even with her, but it was fun all the time.

And so, one trip ended and another came into view. This time, Patty went to visit her family in Berkeley and I went with Harry Bauer, Albert W. Harris, Reg. Peck, and Ted Miller for another lion hunt in which I did not share in the chase but had a much more thrilling part.

The second day after our arrival, the dogs found a very hot scent and gave tumultuous chase in which I did take part very briefly. My horse dashed through some head-high brush and, before I could get a look ahead, went down over a two-foot drop-off that gave me such a wrench in the groin that I was grounded for two days, staying in camp and applying copious rubbings of Absorbine Junior.

By the fifth day I was still very sore, but I decided to take a horse and a movie camera and go out, hoping that I might find my way to the finish if the dogs sent a lion up along the ridge as usually happened. I guided my horse at an easy walk along the ridge while the rest of the party descended noisily into the gorge with the dogs. They were soon out of hearing range and I meandered along very slowly with fading hope of much success.

It must have been a half hour later that I heard a faint whoop from the blood-hound. I pulled over to the edge of the ravine, dismounted and tied my horse. I then walked slowly along with the movie camera. By now, there began to be unmistakable

The rest of my angling career would be in loving competition with a wife who was an expert.

sounds that the dogs were on a track and perhaps a mile away but coming closer. In seconds, however, the hub-bub was directly below me and definitely coming my way.

I unsheathed the camera and hung it around my neck. I also eased the holster of my forty-five Colt automatic to a position where I could reach it quickly in case I got too intimate with a fleeing lion. With that, the dogs came in sight and there, leaping into a jack-pine thirty feet down the steep slope, was a large tom lion very much out of breath and looking very mean! I eased down the slope until I was on a level with the lion perched in the tree, and not more than thirty feet straight in front of me. I stood there and ran about fifty feet of sixteen millimeter film with the lion performing as if he had been trained for months for this particular event.

He looked down at the dogs making whoopee about twenty feet below him, then he looked at me with an expression that was distinctly not an invitation to friendship. After a few minutes he stopped his frantic panting and changed his position on the branch as if planning where he would spring to the ground. Then, after giving me one more dirty look, he did just that and outran the dogs for a hundred yards to a very much larger tree which he climbed and perched himself in a huge crotch about twenty feet above the ground.

By now the hunters came on the scene and, after tying up the dogs for their own safety, we all gathered around while Harry nocked his heaviest hunting arrow in his stout yew bow and let fly. I stood behind Harry adding footage to our now precious movie.

The arrow entered just below the lion's shoulder. He reared backwards and fell to the ground; rolled fifty feet to the bottom of the ravine, then crawled into a huge sandstone cave. Harry nocked another arrow and was about to let fly when the lion rolled off a little ledge at the back of the cave, stony dead from the mortal wound of the first arrow which had broken off against his shoulder blade and severed a main artery. Then, as usual, the dogs were turned loose and allowed to pretend that they were responsible for the kill.

We returned to the Pyle Ranch on Tuesday, October 29th, 1929. Little did we know, however, that our carefree crash descent down over the Mogollon Rim was matched by a market crash which would make 1929 a byword in financial history.

It was not until Wednesday evening, as we sat around the supper table, that Floyd Pyle got his radio in action and the stock market proceedings of the day began to come on the air. It would take a priceless bit of stage acting to reproduce the facial expressions of that group as the quotes expanded. Here we sat: Albert W. Harris, Chairman of the Board of Harris Trust and Savings Bank, one of the largest financial institutions in the Midwest, Harry Bauer, a Director of Southern California Edison Company, C. L. Peck, Los Angeles building contractor, Ted Miller son of the Chairman of the Board of the Edison Company— listening to stock quotations that bore no resemblance to what we all knew as "current" prices. At first we were utterly incredulous but that fond illusion was very soon swept away by the unmistakable evidence that this was "for real" and was the first shattering blast of a world's record financial depression in the making.

Fortunately, no one in this group was a margin speculator. Nevertheless, the financial responsibilities of each one were very considerable. Needless to say, the "bears" mentiond in the ensuing conversation were not the kind that have hides that are made into rugs. At the moment, however, nothing could be done except make plans for a prompt departure on Thursday morning, and that we all did.

Among many other trips and projects during these years, I must mention my first go at the steelhead fishing on the Lower Rogue River of Oregon. This trip was important in my life for two reasons; it gave me the friendship of Henry W. O'Melveny through whom I learned to love and cultivate daffodils; and it introduced me to the steelhead fishing of Oregon which netted ten years of the most precious companionship with my wife in

Ken, with a ten-pound steelhead "for rent."

Deadly competition made it fun. The sign says, "This fish rented for the occasion from Kenyon Reynolds."

The flower show on the Terrace at Kencott.

deadly competition that made it fun. And above all, because it eventually involved associations in my religious career which shaped the remainder of my life.

The Wind-at-my-Back was gently guiding me to Oregon where He had plans for me far removed from steelhead fishing. It was just one more of the many threads in the hand of God, so innocent at their first appearance in the tapestry of life.

On the week end of Washington's Birthday, 1931, Mr. O'Melveny invited the Rogue River party of the previous fall to visit his ranch in the San Gabriel Canyon near Los Angeles. It was there that I first became acquainted with the amazing beauty and variety of that courageous little flower, the daffodil. I was irrevocably hooked for the fancy and made a list immediately from the catalogs on Mr. O'Melveny's desk. I held my breath a little as I topped the list with one bulb of John Evelyn at twenty dollars and one of the buff-tinted Tunis at ten dollars. But Patty egged me on and so it became chronic for both of us.

By 1931 our garden had reached a stage of maturity that attracted many visitors. We loved to have them share it with us. In March we staged a garden flower show for the Pasadena Garden Club. We had cut flowers arranged in buried cans on the terraces. It was laughable to hear the comments of the visitors, wondering how we managed to have all those plants in bloom at the same time.

The story of all these months packed with what St. John the Apostle would call the "joys of the world" might make it seem that the threads of God's tapestry were broken but that is not so! There was a huge difference between the thought pattern of Ken Reynolds of those hectic business days, and the thought pattern of the same Ken Reynolds ever so busily engaged in the carefree joys of archery, gardening, angling or just living.

As a matter of fact, it was precisely in these days and in the rapid happenings of this leisure that my thoughts most often wandered back to that terrific night fifteen years earlier which we had spent in a snowdrift, or that summer evening when Patty had asked how the Protestant Churches had fulfilled the promises of Christ; or when the same ideas were expressed in the sermons and conversations at the time of the death of my brother Graham.

On most occasions when these thoughts came to me, I was inclined to set them aside with the mental plea that there must be some suitable answer. I accepted as proof of this the example of the many scholarly and thoughtful non-Catholics whom I knew. There was beginning to be a little voice inside of me, however, that sometimes whispered: aren't you just stalling? Why don't you dig into the question and settle it for yourself on the basis of the evidence presented to you?

I did not learn, however, how vulnerable these thoughts were making me until God played a little trick on me. It happened on the lovely quiet afternoon of Thursday, May 26th, 1932. Jim and Loretta Harvey were invited to have dinner with us at home. There were just the four of us. Jim was taking the afternoon off, so they came early and we sat in the living room having a lovely talk-fest with these our closest and very dear friends.

How God maneuvered to bring the conversation around to religion, I do not know because it was always taboo with us. But God did just that — perhaps through one of Jim's sly Protestant quips. They always made one laugh instead of argue.

Anyway, it was not long before I heard myself framing an answer to somebody's question something like this: "When you come right down to brass tacks, the rewards which the Catholic Church claims to offer and the promises of Christ which she claims to interpret, are so prodigious compared with any and all material values, that a person is really stupid if he does not learn what it takes to qualify *just on the chance that it is all true!*"

I had secretly framed that thought in my mind many times before, but here I had put it into words in the hearing of three pretty important witnesses. Neither they nor I, however, even dreamed that, in these circumstances, they were probably the most important words that ever came out of my head! Life went on ostensibly the same, but God had tied a knot in the tapestry that determined the rest of the fabric.

Chapter 11

ON THE CHANCE THAT IT IS ALL TRUE

I have been delayed a long time before beginning to write this part of my life-story. I can see that God has quietly engineered the delay for a reason. He did not want me to launch into the mystery of His invitation to Faith with nothing but my own case history to describe. He wanted me to wait until I could compare my own approach to the study of the claims of the Catholic Church with that of several other inquirers who had widely different incentives but equally hopeless prospect of success at the start. This has given me precious insights that throw light on my own inquiry.

I have mentioned the matter of *incentive*. In the story of that talk-fest we had with the Harveys, I quoted myself as saying: ". . . a person is stupid not to learn what it takes to qualify just on the chance that it is all true." In these words I was voicing the fact that six years of freedom from preoccupation with the affairs of business had germinated at least the bud of an *incentive* to examine the evidence of Catholic claims.

My promise made to God when we were in danger of freezing to death in the blizzard of 1917 was made from fear. It was not an incentive. My thoughts about Patty's statement of the principal claim of the Catholic Church, made in the summer of 1918, may have planted a seed, but it was not an incentive. But — "rewards worth more than all material values put together?" — that sounded like an incentive — IF TRUE!

Just thirty years later than that Thursday afternoon in May, 1932, a young man came to see me with his fiancee. She was a widow with four lovely Catholic children. He wanted to be instructed in the doctrine of the Catholic Church. *His* incentive was appreciation of the responsibility of becoming the foster-father of those Catholic children. It had nothing to do with the doctrine itself or its benefit to himself.

In response to his request, I indulged in a few seconds of secret reminiscing. I vividly recalled my incentive in 1932. Then I answered: "I will be glad to help you learn the doctrine, but I'd rather try to show you why it is worth learning."

The faintest trace of impatience crossed his face but a look at his fiancee stemmed his annoyance and they sat down.

For two hours I talked about the amazing goodness of God in making this world and putting us in it. I talked about the proof of God's love that He had offered us. I talked about God's invitation to seek the treasure of everlasting life and the help He would give us to harvest that treasure. Yes, I talked about the rewards which the Catholic Church claimed to offer — so prodigious that it would make one want to try to qualify just on the chance that it was all true.

Michael asked a few questions which were definitely skeptical but at the end he thanked me courteously and said they would come back next week. So, we had another two-hour session on the motive for faith. In the middle of the third meeting, however, after five hours of boosting the treasure on my part, Michael said with some embarrassment and therefore with absolute sincerity: "Father Bede, I want you to understand me a little better; I don't believe anything you have told me so far. I can't see any reason to believe that this world, and man in it, is anything but perfectly natural phenomenon that we are using by virtue of man's intelligence. I don't believe that my soul has any properties that could not be shared by a good smart hunting dog."

My thought was: "What a pitifully hopeless prospect for a father of a Catholic family." My reply was: "Michael, I admire your candor and I admit that you are consistent but, if what I have been telling you *is* true, it is surely worth a try. If you are willing to stay with it, I will try to get nearer to your point of view."

By that time, in spite of opposite poles of viewpoint, we had begun to like each other personally so Michael agreed to continue. His incentive was his love for Angela. It had nothing to do with the goal I was proposing. But, his loyalty made it sufficient for another try. For me, it was immensely discouraging! Twice I sounded out other priests to try to get a substitute for my apparently futile efforts. Meanwhile, we kept doggedly at it. It was not until sixteen weeks later, however, that I had the faintest clue that there was hope.

Michael said: "Father Bede, I can't understand why you were so patient back there when I was holding forth about God looking on while man works out his destiny in this world!"

So, God had come to the rescue of His almost vanquished minister and provided Michael an incentive of God's grace!

Michael and Angela are now among the happiest and most devoted Catholics that it has been my privilege to know. It never would have happened, however, without Michael's incentive to stay with it — come what may!

How different it was with me in May of 1932. I was a Militant Protestant Episcopalian. I knew a little about Catholic doctrine. I believed that much of it was invented to keep a strangle-hold on the laity. But — there were those promises of Christ: "Lo, I am with you all days even to the consummation of the world." — "The gates of hell shall not prevail against it." There was the obvious fact of continuity. I knew the Protestant answers, but how could they be reconciled with these promises? I had stalled at this point for twenty years. Something inside me said: "Ken, you called yourself stupid if you delay any longer; what are you going to do about it?"

Then it blossomed in a telephone call. I learned that Father James O'Shea who had preached that sermon at Graham's funeral was now assistant at St. Brendan's Church in Los Angeles, twelve miles away. That would help to keep it secret. I was still very skeptical but the incentive was compelling so I made an appointment with Father O'Shea for the following day.

From what I remember of my approach, it is amazing that Father O'Shea did not tell me that he was too busy to be bothered with me. Today, however, I would secretly chortle with glee to have an inquirer present himself as I did.

I introduced myself as a younger brother of Father Graham Reynolds and said quite frankly that I had come to Father O'Shea because I liked the sermon he preached at Graham's funeral three years earlier.

Then I said: "You probably remember my wife, Patty Reynolds, at St. Andrew's Parish in Pasadena. I believe she is a Catholic saint. The priest who married us seventeen years ago did not try to convert me because he knew that I really worked at my Episcopalian faith. That is the way it has been ever since. I still work at my faith and I believe it.

"I doubt very much if I could ever be a Catholic because there are many points of doctrine which seem to have been added by the Church and I see no reason to believe them. I know, however, that the Catholic Church claims to be the sole gateway provided by God to enable people to get to heaven. I know that she claims to teach all the doctrine taught by Christ to the Apostles. I know that she claims infallible power to defend this doctrine against those who disagree. I know that she claims to have the power to forgive sins and to bring God Himself in Person to her people in the Mass and Communion.

"I resent the fact that the Church is so uncompromising about all these claims, especially the claim of infallibility. It amounts to saying: 'I am right and everybody else is wrong.' But still and all, the only really important thing about life in this world is that it is the place to earn heaven. And since heaven is forever and life is only a few minutes, the reward is infinite and the price, in comparison, is nothing.

"On the other hand, the objections to the Catholic Church and the claims of the other Churches make a hodgepodge out of the whole thing. It does not seem possible that God would let it be so hard to find the answer. I do wish that you would help me to find the answer because I do want to qualify!"

I have no idea what Father O'Shea's thoughts were when I vouchsafed these condescending words of wisdom. I mean it, however, when I say that I would welcome them now with glee, exasperating though they would be to a young priest. After all, they do voice the only perfect incentive. Its goal is infinite.

Whatever may have been his thoughts, Father O'Shea did consent to discuss the matter with me and we arranged to meet on two afternoons per week until I found the answer. He gave me a penny Catechism which I pocketed and went home.

I told Patty that I had called on Father O'Shea and planned to go twice a week to learn about the Catholic Church. I added, however, that I doubted if I could become a Catholic and would rather not talk about it. That was heartless, but it was important because it started Patty on a campaign of prayer!

As for the Catechism, I secretly stuffed it in the back pocket of my work pants and memorized it page by page as I worked in the garden. I did not mention it to Patty although I am sure she would have condoned that little spurt of perfectionism. Undoubtedly, too, the Catechism spread useful seeds in my soul. But all the time I was like a terrier at a rat-hole. I sought the answer to the one question: "My quest is salvation; how does God intend that it should be earned?"

I gradually began to argue with Father O'Shea about points of doctrine in the Catechism. And what is more, I did begin to see the answer to some of these points. I was grateful for a better understanding of what I called the "worship" of the Blessed Virgin. It hinged on an understanding of the abyss between the divine and the human. Christ alone is God-and-Man, bridging the abyss. Mary has no divine power but immense permission to intercede for the gifts of divine bounty. She is the loving hostess at the banquet of graces provided solely by God. Her role is to help souls to love her Son.

But this did not answer my problem. True Christ alone is Incarnate God. He came to earth to bring salvation to all men and to tell them how to share in it. He must have done it in a way that would not confuse the ordinary man or even a docile child.

But the kaleidoscope of present Christianity certainly seemed to be confusing to almost everybody.

Of course, I knew the Protestant answer was that the chosen ministers of the Catholic Church had eventually betrayed the promises of Christ. This left the Protestant Churches and the Orthodox Church carrying on what the Catholic Church had destroyed. This made these Churches the continuation of the true Apostolic Church. The more I thought about this answer, however, the more uncomfortable I felt about attributing such an indefinite identity to a divine Founder and Guardian. But what could be a better answer?

In desperation, I went to the Assistant Pastor of my own Church. He preached interesting sermons and I thought he might fortify my answer. But instead of fortifying it, he simply reviewed it as I had done a hundred times before. He then gave me a little book entitled: Plain Reasons Why You Should Not Join The Church of Rome, by Canon Littledale, a contemporary of Cardinal Newman who obviously did not follow Newman into the Roman Church.

I dashed home with it, exultant that at last I had something tangible. But, alas, as I read it I discovered that it never broached the question to which I sought an answer. It merely blasted doctrine in a way which displayed woeful disregard of the true teaching of the Catholic Church. The worthy Canon's tirade against what I already knew to be true did more to persuade me of the truth of Catholic doctrine than any book I had read before. But it did not help me one iota to answer the question: "How can two Churches teaching opposite things as true, both be the true Church founded by Christ who is God?"

I had been toying for some time with the notion of going to call on a fallen-away priest whom I knew. I thought that he if anyone, could tell me the true answer against the Catholic Church. I mentioned this to Father O'Shea and he concurred. His thought, however, was probably less than enthusiastic!

I went and was very kindly received. I then explained to this priest the nature of my problem. It is interesting to recall what followed. For almost an hour I sat facing him across his desk while he quietly expounded a mixture of philosophy and religion tailor made to fit the poor man's conscience. He argued that salvation resulted entirely from each individual's contact with God through the prompting of the Holy Spirit. He said that he had definitely established a "listening-post" where God made known to him His pleasure.

Then, changing the subject entirely, he said: "From what you tell me I think you must believe that Christ is God and that the Gospel proves that He founded a visible Church. If that is what you believe, there is no place for you except in the Catholic Church."

When I reported this piece of information to Father O'Shea, he amplified it in a way that I shall never forget. Quoting Saint Augustine, he said: "The Church of God came into being when God took human nature in the womb of the Virgin Mary. It was perfect then and embraced all humanity of all time. Christ, in His lifetime, provided all its visible and physical attributes and tools. It functions now by His Spirit and will continue for all time.

"The Church today is a continuation of Christ Himself made possible in a way that only God could devise and provide. It consists of two principal elements, equally necessary. First, the prolongation of His words by means of a continuing body of ordinary men supernaturally and divinely equipped with all the truth which God wished to have taught to the rest of men. He made certain of the protection of this truth by choosing one man to be the Vicar of His very Self, supernaturally empowered to govern and direct those chosen with him to carry forward the word. All of these men would be like other men in human frailty. They would be protected supernaturally only as necessary to keep the Church free from error.

"The second principal element provided by Christ was a marvelous union of the divine and supernatural with the visible and tangible. It was the gift of Sacrament and Sacrifice to bring His saving power to all future generations. There were seven Sacraments to give supernatural provision for all the needs of men. Then Christ crowned all this at the Last Supper with His Apostles by an all-but-unbelievable gift. His redeeming Sacrifice and His own Body and Blood were to be made present for all men for all time. Those who believe and enter in by these Sacraments and this Sacrifice are welcome to the God-provided means of salvation. It is not by any means an easy way but it is made easy by this union with God Himself. Many are proving that it can be done.

"Those who trust God and believe His word, He welcomes. Those who trust only self He will not compel. God, however, does not expect the impossible. He does not exclude those who do not have full access to the Truth. There is one body of Truth, one redeeming Sacrifice, one sacramental source of Fortitude. All who enter heaven must use it — perhaps some quite unaware."

Needless to say, I went home very thoughtful that day.

One thing kept pestering me the next day, as I worked in the garden. What about that uncompromising claim of infallibility? The more I thought about it, the more it seemed that everything hung on that one question. No one could be a Protestant unless he denied the doctrine of infallibility. To believe that the Roman Catholic Church has God's infallible guarantee as custodian of the means of salvation provided by God and to refuse to belong to it posed an intellectual absurdity. It was certainly within the realm of possibility on God's part. But how can we know? My next session with Father O'Shea, I resolved, would be a battle to the death on that question — and so it almost proved to be!

It was a long session and a very animated one but in the end it all boiled down to four items inviting belief in the doctrine of infallibility:

First: its congruity with what we know about the nature of God. He is omnipotent. Salvation is of infinite importance to each individual soul. When we consider what God did to bring us His Revelation and our salvation, it is impossible to believe that He would make it less than certain for us to know.

Second: there is Christ's promise that He would make it certain, recorded in Scripture. Everything in all the Gospels points to Christ's intention as to the unity and continuity of His commission to His first Bishops. This was made specific in His final command recorded by St. Matthew: "Go, therefore, and make disciples of all nations . . . teaching them to observe whatever I have commanded you: and lo, I am with you throughout all time, even to the consummation of the world." The words "whatever I have commanded you" were made into a specific reality by Christ's earlier words recorded by St. John: "The Holy Spirit, whom the Father will send in My name, will in His turn make everything plain, and recall to your minds everything I have said to you." This is God's guarantee of the sum-total of Revelation which Christ brought from heaven. Christ then added His own guarantee that He would be with His Church and keep it one until the consummation of the world.

The third item seemed to me to be the most potent of all: its utter necessity for unity of faith. One glance at the disunity of Protestantism proves that uniformity is impossible without it. Furthermore, all of the seeds of deviation within the Church have been sown in denial of it.

And the fourth item: It has worked! There is nothing taught by the Catholic Church today unless it can be identified in substance with what has always been taught by the Church since it came from the Apostles.

All of these items must, of course, be denied by non-Catholics. But they did seem to remain rather potent in the face of a lot of battering!

As I took my leave, Father O'Shea gave me a book written in 1918 by Father Daniel Lyons, S.J., in Denver, Colorado. The title was: Christianity And Infallibility—Both or Neither.

When I secreted myself next day to devour this book, my first reaction was one of revolt. Its three hundred pages presented such a prodigious array of arguments in such a tone of compulsion and with such a withering refutation of opposition that my unsympathetic dander seemed to shout: "You can't push me around that way!" The more I read, however, the more something inside me was beginning to whisper: "If Christ is God, His promises cannot be subject to failure." I was beginning to *want* to believe.

In other words, my original natural incentive had kept me at it for more than a year and, let's face it, grace was beginning to work. This was, indeed, the crucial combat of my life. I had kept at it from the beginning "on the chance that it may be true". Now, I had studied the evidence and God was inviting me to make one decision which was just a little beyond the reach of reason alone. I was invited to take God's word for it on the basis of evidence that God had chosen to give.

And here again I stand in awe of the ingenuity of God's Providence. He was providing in minute detail the atmosphere for a right choice without the crudity of compulsion. I have often wondered how long I would have drifted on in combat had it not been for that new-found sense of nearness to God that stemmed from my work in the garden.

As 1933 got under way, my precious new varieties of daffodils began to bloom and I began, for the first time, to do some cross-pollenizing. The thing that made it fun for me was the thought of God's all-important part in creating new varieties of daffodils from seed. I had been through so many heartaches in trying to perfect new ideas in gasoline plant equipment that God's perfect success with every try kept me fascinated. Patty and I had been making crosses from mid-January into April. We, or at least I, had plenty of time among these courageous little flowers to think about God.

As our last crosses were tagged and recorded, we decided to go into the Northwest where the daffodil season would be just beginning. We started out on April 17th and spent the first night with Mother and Dad at their new little cottage on their old farm at Gustine, California. Next day we drove leisurely to Berkeley arriving early in the afternoon to stay the night with Dr. Bill and Minerva Donald at their beautiful new North Berkeley home.

Memory is a strange companion. As I look back at that brief visit, I remember three minutes of it as if it were yesterday. The rest is almost a blank. But those minutes were planned by God. I was coming down from the guest-room on the second floor just after sunset and stopped on the landing before a large view-window looking west across San Francisco Bay and on out the Golden Gate.

That evening it really was the *Golden* Gate. The sky fairly blazed into the copper gold of the bay and the sea beyond the Gate. The setting was dramatic but that was only incidental. It was during the next two minutes that I came the nearest to a true supernatural experience that I have ever known. The grandeur and the power and the tender love of God seemed to overwhelm me. All my years of conflicting thoughts converged into the notion that Christ was saying to me: "Kenyon, what are you waiting *for*?" It was not quite as drastic as St. Paul's experience at the gate of Damascus but its effect in me was similar. There are no words in any language which can make it describable.

God, being a pure Spirit, is intimately close to us but just beyond the reach of our natural grasp. My natural spirit had wrestled with the natural evidence that God offers to reason. Now, at last, I was beginning to see the utter adequacy of God Himself—past all human power of judging. It is something that cannot be expressed in words—and yet, there is no doubt in my mind that, during those minutes, God Himself opened the door of my soul and let my will have access to a supernatural grasp of Truth which really bears no relation to natural faith. It is a way of knowing that does not decide—it takes God's word for it. Since that day, I can see the abyss of difference between natural faith and supernatural faith. The one can and should weigh the evidence and decide — the other *has* weighed the evidence and knows the answer. And, until this day, it startles me to see how many people seem to confuse the two.

Excuse me for keeping you on that stair-landing for so long! But my life has been very different since that event. My first thought was to dash to the telephone and call Father O'Kelly and ask him to give me conditional baptism forthwith. But second thought was a little more prudent. Father O'Kelly knew nothing about these goings-on during the seventeen years since he had married us. Furthermore, I had placed myself under instruction with Father O'Shea and should be guided by his advice. I decided that I was safe in God's hands until I could consult with my instructor.

Why, or how, I kept all this from Patty I have no idea. It amazes me now as something utterly foreign to the rest of our life together. As far as I know, we never had any other secrets from each other. But somehow she never had a clue that I was a captive of Christ from that day on.

We did continue our trip and spent several happy days consulting with daffodil growers in Oregon. But I was increasingly impatient to reach home and there to consult with Father O'Shea. We returned to Kencott on Friday, May 5th, 1933. Next day I hastened to present myself at St. Brendan's Rectory. I was taken aback, however, when I disclosed my sudden change of heart, to find Father O'Shea not altogether enthusiastic for my immediate baptism. Perhaps his reaction was the result of a very busy Saturday morning in a big parish, but more likely it was in confirmation of the prudence which God had inspired in me together with His gift of grace on that stair-landing in Berkeley. In any case, God, as usual, was managing the matter, and from that time on, for the rest of my life His decisions were directives for me!

I borrowed a small paperback Missal which I could secrete in my pocket and began to memorize all the "common" of the Mass in Latin so I could watch the ceremony without a book and know what was going on.

My sessions with Father O'Shea continued twice each week until, on Monday, June 26th, he suggested that the following Friday, June 30th, the commemorative feast of St. Paul the Apostle, would be a good day for me to be received into the Catholic Church.

I hastened home and found Patty waiting for me on the terrace as I came down the steps from the garage. I said: "Prepare yourself for a shock — Father O'Shea is going to receive me into the Church next Friday." For a second I thought that she was going to faint, but it was not from shock. I honestly do not know what her thoughts were or how much she had suspected. She said, however, that she had about given up hope when she saw in my desk the copy of Canon Littledale's Plain Reasons Why You Should Not Join The Church Of Rome. Then, suddenly, it came to both of us what a precious gift it was for *us*. How it did change everything! Not outwardly, but within. Our souls were knit together as never before. And that never changed again.

And so we assembled within the rather bleak concrete walls of the unfinished baptistry at St. Andrew's Church on the Feast of St. Paul. Loretta Harvey was proxy for Lawrence vander Leck as Godfather. Jessie, God bless her, attended with ill-restrained tears at my "apostacy". But I was grateful that she came since I remembered how I felt when Graham left my Church some twenty years earlier.

What a whale of a difference it made! that little item of God's supernatural gift of grace! I received conditional Baptism; made Profession of Faith and then received conditional absolution in the confessional. Then, on Saturday, the Feast of the Most Precious Blood of Christ, I received my First Communion.

Daffodils in the rock garden at Kencott.

Chapter 12

HAPPILY EVER AFTER

After telling this story of my conversion, I cannot help thinking: "What more is there to say except that threadbare old cliche, 'and they lived happily ever after'?" Indeed, cliche or not, that would precisely state the truth.

But the tapestry of God's plan was only well begun. He was now inviting Patty and me as a team to take up other threads to complete a far different picture.

Ostensibly, life went on much the same. There was the same round of travel to Coffee Pot Lodge, to the Rogue, North Umpqua, McKenzie and Eel Rivers for hunting and fishing. There were many daffodil trips. One of these involved a six-thousand mile tour of England, Scotland, Wales, Ireland and Holland visiting hybridizers and daffodil shows. It was another delightful trip with a *quest.* We returned with one hundred new varieties of daffodils and many new friends.

The same joyous awareness of the treasure of our new unity of faith pervaded everything we did. We thought nothing of going fifty or more miles, Sunday after Sunday, when our fishing trips took us that far away from a church. I was also naively forgetful of the necessity of an incentive to encourage the rest of my family to investigate my discovery of Faith. I broached the idea to each one of them and found them just as cold as I would have been without that precious incentive.

There was, however, one exception — my brother-in-law Colonel Fred Terrell. The one adjective that comes to mind regarding the United States Infantry Officers of the early decades of this century is "hard-boiled". Indeed it is appropriate insofar as it might result from exposure to hardship, suffering and human savagery. Fred had a generous share of all of it during the Moro uprising in the Philippine Islands in the early nineteen

Ken looking over his daffodil seedlings in the tea house at Kencott.

hundreds and again in France in World War One. It was in France that exposure to gas attacks gave him a lifelong legacy of suffering.

It was only my brand new Catholic exuberance that gave me the notion to broach the subject to Fred when I was visiting at his bedside during one of his severe gas-aggravated attacks of asthma. I was really taken by surprise when Fred leaned toward me and said: "Ken, I believe you are dead right. I have known for a long time that the Catholic Church must have something that no other Church can match. It takes more than natural courage for those Army Chaplains to expose themselves the way they do for their boys in the field."

Here again was incentive independent of doctrine. The upshot of it was that I brought Father O'Shea to Fred's bedside and on July 12th, 1935, he was received into the Church.

And so more fishing and gardening years passed by until 1937 became for us, really and truly, a "year of grace". God wasted no time in getting it started. It was announced at St. Andrew's Church in Pasadena that, on Sunday, January 10th, the Paulist Father, John Handly, would begin what was called a "Rosary Novena". Each day for twenty-seven days there would be Mass in the morning and a sermon and Rosary in the evening.

With that announcement, an idea slipped into my mind, or was slipped there by somebody's guardian angel. As a result, after consulting with Patty, I wrote to Mother Pfitzer telling her that Patty and I intended to "make" the Novena in behalf of Irma, Patty's sister, who had been nine years in a sanitarium.

I enclosed a Rosary with full instructions how to use it and invited Mother to join us in her home at the same hour. I knew that Mother was vulnerable because, ever since Joe's death in 1921, she had gone to Mass with Dad quite regularly. The invitation to pray the Rosary for Irma just might be the "last straw", and it certainly would not arouse opposition.

With that, Patty and I launched on our first and only Rosary Novena. Father Handly was absolutely unique. He was a Tennessean who had spent one bleak winter in New England. The sight of women, old and young, plodding through the snow at six a.m. to go to Mass gave him *his* incentive and, as Graham had predicted of me, "when he fell, he fell hard."

His Southern droll wit and his simplicity made him invincible. I liked him immediately and invited him to our home several times during the Novena. We became devoted friends and exchanged letters almost every week until he died nine years later. His spiritual guidance did much to shape my life; another maneuver of God's goodness for which I am grateful.

The Rosary Novena ended on February 5th. In his sermon Father Handly just hinted at the hope that some of us who had attended daily Mass for twenty-seven days would find it possible to continue. That was the most precious hint that ever came my way. That night I set the alarm as usual for six a.m. but I was awake before it exploded so I shut it off and said to Patty, "I am making no promises and setting no precedent and I don't want you to feel any urge on my account, but I am going to Mass."

"I just hoped that you would", was Patty's reply.

And with that, we went to Mass together. It was an experiment but it continued. It was not long until it was taken for granted by both of us that breakfast might be skipped, but never the precious privilege of daily Mass and Communion. And thus it became a lifelong treasure for both of us.

So, God having opened 1937 by making us daily-Communicants, used that fact to further other plans. While the thrill of wet-fly fishing for steelhead had won our loyalty, the finesse and art of dry-fly fishing at Coffee Pot Lodge had always remained our first love. But at Coffee Pot Lodge there was no Catholic Church within reach even during the summer months. As a result, we gradually transferred our interest to the much more beautiful McKenzie River in Oregon. There, at McKenzie Bridge, we found a public resort, Log Cabin Inn, that provided almost a duplicate of the arrangement we had at our own Coffee Pot Lodge. We made two trips to Log Cabin Inn in 1937 and toward the end of our second visit we were having lunch with our friends Frances and Fred Burnham.

North Bank Farm when we first saw it in 1937.

Fred remarked, "Ken, I wish you would go over on North Bank Road this afternoon before you go to Gordon's on the North Umpqua. There is a place for sale over there that would just suit you for a summer home."

"O.K. Fred," I said, "I need another summer home about like I need a pet camel, but I'll take a look."

So, while Patty was getting ready for the trip to North Umpqua, Fred and I went over to call on the dear little lady at North Bank Farm. She was quite frank and told us of the trials she had been through when her husband went to the hospital the year before. And now she wanted to go to be near him.

I asked her what price she was asking and she replied: "I would like to get five thousand dollars. It cost us a good deal more than that but I realize that prices are down now."

Here was forty acres with fourteen hundred feet of the McKenzie River. Not only did ownership include the bed of the river, but it included a three acre island six hundred feet long opposite the house. There was a water tower, a small garage and a work-shop and about eight acres of garden around the house. The rest was fir and cedar forest.

It was true that prices were still at low ebb in July of 1937. But at that price I figured it was about like putting the money in the bank. I knew that I had a dozen friends who would snatch it if I decided not to keep it.

So, I dashed back to Log Cabin Inn and telephoned to Gordon's that we would not arrive until the following day. Then Patty and I returned for another look. We spent a couple of hours and walked over the whole place. There was no doubt about our mutual delight with all of it. The only hitch was the distance to a church.

That evening, a fantastic idea began to percolate in my mind which I refrained from putting into words. It must have been put there by God because I did not have the foggiest idea how it could be carried out.

Next morning, however, when Patty and I were on our way to Roseburg and the North Umpqua, I said: "The Frothingham

The bridge at the island at North Bank Farm.

Patty makes a perfect cast, (you can see the line and the fly).

Big Rock Pool on the North Umpqua. Patty's skillful casting brought results.

place is fifty-four miles from the nearest church; it wouldn't suit us for a permanent place unless —"

"unless McKenzie Bridge becomes a metropolis?" chimed in Patty with a sly chirp.

"No!" I insisted, "unless some kind of a religious community could be persuaded to locate there."

"Just who," said Patty, "would locate so far from people? They all have their houses near the people they serve."

"Well, how about retired priests or those doing special research or those who are devoted to prayer; don't they have what they call cloistered communities of monks and nuns? I could write to Father Handly and he would tell me the possibilities. What do you say we buy it and then do a little prospecting? We could easily get our money back if it fell through."

"I think you're a darling starry eyed dreamer", countered Patty, "but it's O.K. by me if you want to try it."

With that, I pressed the throttle a little deeper and, when we reached Roseburg, I hied to the telephone office, called up Frances Burnham, and asked her to go over to tell Mrs. Frothingham that we would buy the place. I added that I was mailing a check for an option.

During the next four days at Gordon's Steamboat Lodge we had plenty to think about beside the Umpqua steelhead fishing although that was excellent. Then, I opened an account at the bank in Eugene, Oregon and arranged with Judge Lawrence T. Harris to negotiate the Frothingham purchase.

Next, we made a three-day trip to Carmel to witness the marriage of Patty's brother Alan to Barbara Gale of Berkeley. Those present were Alan, Barbara, Patty, myself, and the priest, standing for ten minutes by the vesting table in the sacristy. What a pity, I thought, that a mixed-marriage must be so drab. Bobby is a very lovely girl and certainly won't find this coldness inviting.

A few days after we returned to Kencott, the mailman brought me a letter that I opened with puzzlement and read with even greater wonder as to how-come. It was plainly addressed to *MR.*

Kenyon L. Reynolds and contained a brief note from Mother telling me that she wanted to talk to me and hoped that I could come to Berkeley soon. Patty and I dared to hope that this might have something to do with that Rosary Novena of last January, and so it turned out.

I never have figured out just why Mother asked for me alone without Patty. Perhaps it was to prove to herself that it was entirely her own will without the bolstering that Patty had always given her.

Whatever her thoughts may have been, Mother soon took me aside and said, "Do you know, Kenny, when you sent me that Rosary and told me that you and Hazel were praying for Irma, I wanted to join you and I did. But when it came to saying in the Creed, 'I believe in the Holy Catholic Church', I said to myself, 'That's not true; I don't believe in the Catholic Church', and I didn't want to say it. But I kept on on account of Irma. Then, one Sunday I was praying the Rosary at Mass and when I recited the Creed, I just thought, 'I do believe and I want to receive Christ in Communion.' So, that is why I asked you to come so you could tell me what to do."

The first thing I did was to take her in my arms and thank God for His blessed goodness. Then, I telephoned to Father O'Kelly who was now Pastor of the Church of St. Theresa, the Little Flower, in Oakland. We called on him and he, after questioning Mother carefully, baptized her and received her into the Church with me as witness. Next morning we all went to the Little Flower Church so Mother could receive her First Communion from Father O'Kelly.

And so the example of my darling Patty in her uphill struggle to maintain her steadfast faith had won another convert; first her father, then her brother, then her husband, and last of all her mother — but there were still more to come.

Father Handly was our house-guest in September and I told him of our project. He expressed the wish that the Paulist Fathers could be the beneficiaries of my scheme but did not see how it could be worked. He suggested, however, that when title

North Bank Farm rechristened St. Benedict Lodge, June 28, 1940.

was secured, I should write to various religious institutions and make an offer. He seemed optimistic of success.

On February 5th, 1938, title deed was recorded in Lane County records transferring North Bank Farm from Frances A. Frothingham to Kenyon L. Reynolds and Hazel P. Reynolds, husband and wife! — and thus began a thrilling final chapter in the lives of said husband and wife in which God's hand is obvious.

In fact, God gave the first cue toward following Father Handly's advice. It came in the form of a well phrased appeal from Rev. Justine Snyder, O.S.B. for a contribution for an Indian Mission project at Stephan, South Dakota. This was a mission of St. Meinrad Abbey of the Order of Saint Benedict located in Indiana. In response to my contribution, I began to receive the Grail Magazine from St. Meinrad Abbey.

I had no idea of the meaning of the letters "O.S.B." after Father Justine's name, nor had I ever heard of Saint Benedict.

But the Grail articles seemed to stem from a large institution. So, when Patty and I finally became the possessors of the deed to North Bank Farm, I wrote to the editor of Grail Magazine. In this letter I explained that I had just acquired ownership of a beautiful piece of property on the McKenzie River in the Coast Mountains of Oregon and I was prepared to finance the building of a chapel and living quarters for a small group of religious people for year-around occupancy. I also explained that my chief interest was to make certain of daily Mass in the vicinity of my summer home.

God's part in the scheme was ill-concealed when the answer came. It disclosed that Mount Angel Abbey, about one hundred miles from McKenzie Bridge, would be the host of the triennial General Chapter in July of 1938. So, for the first time in twenty-seven years, the Abbot of St. Meinrad Abbey would be in Oregon and would be pleased to visit us at McKenzie Bridge.

So, it was in high glee that Patty and I returned to Log Cabin Inn in May and began a feverish campaign of house remodeling, bridge repair, garden planning, brush clearing, plus much fishing and visiting with friends and our own guests. We returned to Kencott in June to harvest daffodils.

On July 7th we were back at Log Cabin Inn in response to a tentative date set by Father Abbot Ignatius Esser of St. Meinrad Abbey. We arrived at 4:00 p.m. and found a letter stating that Father Abbot would arrive that same afternoon. While we were reading the letter, in came a car occupied by two priests whom we hastened to greet. They were soon registered as: Rt. Rev. Ignatius Esser, O.S.B., Abbot, St. Meinrad, Indiana, and Rev. Eugene Medved, O.S.B., Monk of Mount Angel Abbey, St. Benedict, Oregon. These were the first Benedictine Monks Patty and I had ever seen. How little did any of us know what the sequel to that meeting would be!

Like everything that God manages in minute detail, however, the ensuing history of our campaign for daily Mass at North Bank Farm followed a course utterly different from what we humans would call plain sailing. It would be tedious to record in detail the ups-and-downs of our hopes during the next two years. A glimpse, however, will be interesting. Abbot Ignatius was utterly delighted with the whole project BUT it was too far from St. Meinrad Abbey to be practicable. He urged Abbot Thomas Meier of Mount Angel Abbey to take a look. Abbot Thomas did look and the Chapter of Mount Angel Abbey was equally delighted — BUT it was contrary to the interest of the Archdiocese of Portland to sequester so many monks. Abbot Thomas offered, if I would build a chapel and priest's quarters, to supply a monk for Chaplain as long as we lived there — BUT that would necessitate deeding the property to the Archdiocese. A Chaplain might at least be provided for the summer months — BUT that would interfere with the interests of Father Francis Leipzig, Pastor at far away Eugene.

The whole matter was further complicated by the decision of Mount Angel Abbey to send five Monks to Vancouver, British Columbia, to take over the Archdiocesan Seminary there.

So, our joy was considerably dampened as we moved into the rejuvenated North Bank Farm on May 24th, 1939. There seemed to be a stalemate as to the whole prospect of daily Mass.

Then God quietly resolved the whole issue. On June 4th a letter from Father Abbot Thomas announced that the Chapter of Mount Angel Abbey had voted unanimously in favor of promoting the plan for a chapel and priest's quarters and providing a Chaplain. The Abbey then undertook to straighten out the Archdiocesan problem together with Father Leipzig.

On August 27th Father Leipzig notified us that all the difficulties had been resolved and Archbishop Howard of Portland had agreed to allow the Mount Angel Plan to proceed. Once more joy reigned at North Bank Farm as I learned anew that if a matter is left entirely in God's hands, He will come up with a far better answer than our plans could possibly provide. Our dream of a perfect summer home with a chapel and daily Mass was, at last, definitely in the offing. Archbishop Howard had been God's instrument to provide the best possible answer to our hopes.

Then, it happened! On September first Germany invaded Poland and on September 3rd England declared war on Germany and World War Two was on.

So, again, God was asking us to trust Him — come what may! Fortunately for us, however, the war was very remote from Western United States for the first two years. It did not involve us in any way as yet so our lives went on as usual.

We were able to start intensive work on the preparation of the chapel and priest's quarters immediately upon our return to North Bank Farm on April 17th, 1940.

All had proceeded so well that Father Abbot Thomas came down on April 29th to inspect and approve the mighty preparations. The altar for the chapel was finished and installed on May 25th. Finally, on June 19th, we went to Eugene and called on Father Leipzig at the Rectory where our cherished friend, confessor, and Father in Christ, Father Charles Moser, O.S.B. was waiting for us. We reached North Bank Farm in time for dinner and spent a happy evening getting all in readiness. On the following morning our joy can be imagined as Father Charles blessed the house and then offered our first Mass. I served; Patty, her mother and father and Alan assisted and all received Communion together. On Friday morning 7:30 Mass "as usual" was inaugurated and North Bank Farm was re-christened Saint Benedict Lodge, the name it still enjoys today.

On Saturday, June 29th, Alan and Barbara left for Alan's new job at Spokane and we took Mother and Dad to the Portland Airport for their return to Gustine. We returned by way of Mount Angel Abbey to pick up Father Charles who had returned there for a Golden Jubilee Celebration.

In August we went with friends to the Queen Charlotte Islands of British Columbia to sample the fly-fishing for Cohoe Salmon in the Tlell River. It was a delightful experience but is remembered especially because we stopped en route to visit our friends the Benedictine Monks from Mount Angel Abbey. They were moving into new quarters near the city of New Westminster and had chosen the name of Westminster Priory for their Com-

The Cohoes on the Tlell River took fly as if they really meant it.

munity. The monastery was a spacious old residence on the shore of Deer Lake. It was not yet under papal enclosure so we were invited to spend the night in the temporary guest-room which was the master bedroom of the old Buscombe residence.

How utterly amazed and incredulous I would have been if my Guardian Angel had whispered to me: "Five years and three weeks from today you will be scrubbing the floor in this bathroom which will then be the Founding Abbot's suite!" But that night it was only to be admired for its elaborate fixtures.

On our return to St. Benedict Lodge we were dinner guests with our beloved Chaplain. The meal was memorable because of Father Charles' extra-specialty, macaroni-and-Swiss-cheese. It should be world famous! We were rapidly learning how much better for us was this arrangement with one Chaplain than would be a priory with half a dozen monks. They would be sufficient unto themselves and we would see little of them. This way, they were our close friends and semi-guests.

Early 1941 had a trial for us. In February, Dr. Larry Chaffin operated on Patty to remove a large tumor, which, thank God, proved to be benign. Patty made a rather quick recovery, however, so we were able to return to St. Benedict Lodge in mid-April.

This spring and summer were not quite the same as usual. The war in Europe was increasingly menacing. This was emphasized for all of us as we sat around the radio at supper time on May 27th to hear President Roosevelt declare the situation an "unlimited emergency". We were grateful for the comparative peace at St. Benedict Lodge which continued all summer except for the terrible news from outside.

On our return to Kencott in November, we stopped at Fresno, California, where my nephew, Major Fred Terrell, was then stationed. He was flying patrol bombers over the Pacific and returning to the passenger airport with a full load of bombs because they did not have a sufficient supply to risk dropping them in the ocean. He, of course, did not mention that fact to us at the time, but two weeks later was December 7th and "Pearl

Harbor Day" was inaugurated. Then everybody knew that we were caught short.

What a strange situation this was! The United States was suddenly thrust into the most deadly war of the world's history. Psychologically, it was an utterly different world; physically, all we could do was to hastily improvise a blackout and wait. In the daytime everything seemed to go as usual. That, however, only applied to our generation entering their fifties and older.

Pearl Harbor was a double event for the Alan Pfitzer family. At the very hour of that disaster their second daughter, Patricia, came into the world at Tacoma, Washington. Two considerations, Bobbie's poor health, and Alan's decision to enter the Navy, instigated our offer to take their two tiny daughters into our home pending developments.

All was put in readiness at Kencott and, on February 24th, I put Patty on a plane bound for Tacoma. She returned three days later with two-and-one-half-months-old little Patty and three-and-one-half-years-old Joanie to make Kencott a very different place for a few months. Joanie was a very timid little three-year-old at first but it was not long before she felt at home with me. This was proved by the new hyphenated name I gave her which she recited as if it were a ritual: "Barbara-Joan-Faller-Down-Why-Pest-Pfitzer!"

Meanwhile, Alan Morphy and I were sounding out the possibilities of getting back into harness for whatever service we might be able to give to our country at war. After some consultation with my old friends in the oil industry, I was invited to enter the organization hastily being assembled to manage the war-output of the petroleum industry. So, on March 25th, 1942, I became Chief of the Natural Gas and Natural Gasoline Section of District Five of the Petroleum Administration for War, or P.A.W. as it was called, with offices in Los Angeles.

As can be imagined, the activities of this new organization were feverish and demanding. The technical progress of the industry during the sixteen years of my retirement had been so great that I was overwhelmed with anxiety during the first few weeks of my new office. My job required constant dealings with the members of the Natural Gas and Natural Gasoline Industry Committee. Their professional jargon was almost like a foreign language to me. I hadn't the foggiest idea of the meaning of many of their technical terms. In fact, had it not been for the help of many old friends who came to my rescue during those first days, I would have been utterly inadequate for the job. By dint of much 'midnight-oil', however, I began to catch on and, after a few perilous weeks, I could do business as of old.

Thus came the end of a treasure-laden phase of the life of this "Mighty Lucky-Boy". In one sense, it might have seemed selfish and inconsequential. Perhaps God had found it necessary to pamper me far beyond anything I had ever deserved in order to make me vulnerable to His saving grace. Perhaps that is why He ended it in these war years. They provided an interim leading up to a final phase that will let me pay for my "vacation" in the middle of life with a service which is all the more gratefully given. In any case, I shall never cease to thank God for all of it and would not change a day of it!

Chapter 13

FINIS

The last three years of the great and hideous war were filled with new and hectic experiences for me. They were years of the most exacting tenseness of my life. A book should be written about the fascinating energy and coordination of effort which went into the contribution made by the Oil Industry to bring the war to a successful conclusion.

All this involved me in constant study with the men operating in the field in my Division. There were meetings and conferences and decisions to be made. Now and then there were quarrels to be settled and injustices to be made right.

St. Benedict Lodge continued to be a consolation because of its mere existence. Patty was able to spend some time there with our various dear ones. My enjoyment of it, however, was limited to two round trips by air to spend ten days looking after necessities. Daily Mass and Communion was about the only feature of our lives that resembled the past. That kept all the rest in balance as the war ground on to its futile end.

The next big step in my life God withheld until the beginning of the third year of my war service. The first hint of its arrival was just about as innocuous as could well be imagined. It happened as we were dressing to go to Mass on the morning of April 13th, 1944, the date of our departure for a brief stay at St. Benedict Lodge.

Turning toward me from her dressing table, Patty said: "I've got an odd lump on the left side of my throat just below my jawbone. It doesn't hurt but it feels kind of numb. It has been that way for a couple of weeks and doesn't seem to be getting any better."

I felt of the spot she indicated and could feel the little lump of the submaxillary gland that everybody has on each side of the throat. Perhaps the left side was a little larger and a little more knotty.

I said, "We'll get Bill Donald to look at it when we are in Berkeley tomorrow." With that, we went to the six-thirty Mass and I went to the office as usual.

Next morning, Dad Pfitzer met us as we stepped down on the station platform at Berkeley. We went to see Bill Donald at his home. After carefully examining the lump beside Patty's throat, he said, "If it is still bothering when you come back from Oregon, I think you would do well to go and see Larry Chaffin." So, we went on board the "Cascade" for Eugene, relieved that Bill did not seem to think it was very serious.

Everything was so perfect at St. Benedict Lodge that it did not seem possible that there could be so much sorrow in the world. The daffodils were superb. I hardly had time to enjoy them, though, with the many chores which needed doing during the eight days of my stay.

But the war was not over and my job demanded my return. Patty stayed on with guests, so it was May 20th when I met her at Glendale arriving on the "Owl". Patty's throat did not seem to be any worse, but neither was it any better, so we called on Dr. Chaffin and he decided that an operation was advisable. He set the appointment for Wednesday, May 31st.

I took Patty in to the Good Samaritan Hospital on Tuesday evening and returned there next morning after six-thirty Mass at St. Andrew's. I wished Patty a "happy landing" as she was wheeled to the operating room just before eight o'clock. Then I went to the parlor and did a little calculating. I figured that it would not possibly require more than a half-hour to remove that little lump about the size of a hazel-nut from Patty's throat and send her back as good as new.

After the half-hour had edged its way into two hours, my heart became numb with a searching chill. I knew that throat cancer was deadly business. Two of our acquaintances had died within a year after apparently successful operations. But Patty had never smoked in her life; perhaps there was still a chance.

Another two hours, though, of prayer and a desperate attempt at resignation, let me know the answer when Dr. Chaffin returned at noon and said what he had to say.

I can see now why God gave me those four hours of abject and lonely desolation. In fact, it began to dawn on me as I sat there with more than enough time to think.

Here we were, in the very prime of life and up until now looking forward to a post-war paradise with all that the world had to offer. We had every facility to enjoy life; a beautiful home and garden; a summer home such as angels might love; more hobbies than we could keep in hand; more money than we could use. We could do what we pleased and go where we pleased. Above all, we were practically alike in all that we pleased. And now, to crown it all, God had given us equal Faith to love and hope that He be pleased with us . . .

That *He* be pleased with *us*? . . . the meaning contained in that question-mark entered into a good deal of my thought during the last of those four hours. It reminded me of my syllogism for the Catholic Faith: Life is for minutes — salvation is forever: ergo, life is for salvation.

Four hours was a long time to be without a hint as to how the operation was going! I began to wonder if, perhaps, she was already in heaven. If that had happened, the rest of my life was to be aimed at joining her! Then and there, without a trace of presumption, I instituted my "Project Sainthood" and that has been the motive of my life ever since.

And so it was almost an occasion for rejoicing when Larry Chaffin finally came to see me. The serious expression on his face did not, thank God, mean her death. She was a very sick lady after a searching operation to remove every trace of malignant tissue, but the operation had not disclosed a hopeless situation. Her general health should tell in her favor.

When I saw her a few minutes later, I almost wept. She was indeed a very sick lady moaning in a half conscious doze, her face almost hidden in bandaging. I stayed until she was fully conscious and actually tried to put together a smile with a face that was still all but immobilized.

Then I went back to the office and returned later to sit by her bed and re-think the thoughts of the morning. God's part in all of it seemed uppermost. I had ceased entirely to feel that desolation that had haunted the morning hours.

Next morning, Patty was much improved but since the wound was open into her throat, she had to have intravenous feeding and careful hospital attention. So, it was exactly two weeks before she could be allowed to return home and then, with a huge bandage still around her throat. Bandage-and-all, however, we were back together at the six-thirty Mass on June 15th, much to the joy of the dozen or so "regulars" at St. Andrew's Church.

Little did we realize that "June 15th" gave us exactly one more year to go. Neither did we realize that "Project Sainthood" was to make that year, really and truly, the happiest year of our two lives.

The bandage was soon removed and Patty was almost her old self once more. The left side of her face was permanently paralyzed, but the dimple and the smile were all the more attractive on the right side. By the end of July, Patty was ready to return to St. Benedict Lodge.

Things at the office were by now reduced to a semblance of routine so I was able to be absent for the entire month of August. Our stay at St. Benedict Lodge was once more a month of pure joy. Our guests were Jim and Loretta Harvey, Jim's mother and my godson Jimmy Harvey. The presence of Doctor Jim and Father Charles gave a sense of physical and spiritual security that added to the joy. A sense of preciousness of every minute seemed to pervade the doings of all of us. It was not an anxious feeling but just an urge to enjoy this God-given peace to the limit.

After our return to Kencott, Patty resumed her weekly visits to the doctor for a "check-up". He reported her condition as "satisfactory" but I noticed that she was showing signs of frailty. Instead of digging in the garden as of old, she loved to sit on the

Instead of digging in the garden as of old, Patty loved to sit on the terrace and relax.

terrace and relax. This did not, however, keep her from responding enthusiastically when the occasion made it opportune for us to have Barbara Joan and Patty Pfitzer once more as house-guests. Alan was now in training at the Naval Training Base in Florida and this arrangement would enable Barbara to join him there.

So, on December 5th, Barbara arrived at Kencott with her two little daughters, now three and six years old and very vivacious. Barbara took the train for Florida the same evening and our home once more became a lively scene. Patty's frailty, however, began to disturb me so I got well acquainted with my little nieces conniving with them to save my Patty from distress.

Alan and Barbara returned on January 3rd, 1945, and picked up their family en route for Alan's final training at San Diego. Their departure left a tremendous hiatus in our family but I was rather relieved because I knew that Patty no longer felt equal to any exertion.

When I accompanied Patty to Dr. Chaffin's office two weeks later, he came out while Patty was dressing and said: "Ken, I know that you don't want to leave a stone unturned to do all that can be done for your wife's welfare. There is definite evidence of recurrence and I would like to send you to Dr. Hayes Martin at the Memorial Hospital in New York. He is recognized as the leading authority for cancer of the chest and head. I am sure Patty will be safe in his care."

Fortunately, since Larry was Chief Surgeon for the Santa Fe Railway, he was able to get us reservations to New York. We visited dear Father Handly in Chicago and, fortified by his blessing, presented ourselves to Dr. Hayes Martin on the morning of January 31st, 1945. He very promptly decided that an operation was indicated. So, the following afternoon we went to the Memorial Hospital and Patty was given mighty preparations for the operation which was scheduled for eight o'clock next morning.

I arrived an hour ahead of time to give blood for transfusion. Then I went to Patty's room and waited. Just then a nurse entered and said: "Mr. Reynolds is wanted on the telephone in the doctor's office." I felt a strange emptiness clutch at my heart; nobody but Patty and the doctor knew that I was here! And so it turned out. The "telephone" was the doctor in person with a full-size X-ray of Patty's chest showing both lungs infected so there was no chance to operate.

And when I asked for the rest he said, "She might last for three months." Then he added, "You would better tell her that I recommend postponing the operation till after further treatment by Dr. Chaffin."

I replied, "Doctor, you are not a Catholic and I quite understand your suggestion, but a Catholic has a right to know the truth because preparation for death is more important than life.

"You may be right," he said, "but if you tell her, it must be entirely on your own responsibility. Early in my professional life I told one patient. He was a widower with two small children and I thought that there was a practical necessity in his case. He went out and shot himself. I have let others do the telling since then."

With that, we shook hands, he wished me well and we parted. I went and sat on Patty's bed and told her all but the prognosis. It was, perhaps a test of faith for both of us, but to my surprise, we both seemed almost lighthearted. I made a little crack about wasting my blood and Patty, smiling, opined that somebody else was welcome to it. Then Patty dressed and we became momentarily tourists in the "Big City".

It happened that a Church of St. Jude stood across the street from the Memorial Hospital and for the previous two days I had been spending some time there taking part in a Novena to the great Apostle, Patron of Hopeless Cases. I suggested that we make that our first stop and we did. Then we went window-shopping on Fifth Avenue.

The next thing to think about was getting home. We went to see my fraternity brother, Paul Lakin, at the New York office of the Shell Oil Company. Paul made a couple of unsuccessful phone calls and then said, "Ken, why don't you go and call on the Chief Passenger Agent of the Santa Fe at their office here in New York and just tell him the facts? I can get you to Chicago if he will take you from there."

This I did and was very courteously received. I told him exactly the situation and asked for his help to get any kind of space on the Santa Fe from Chicago to Los Angeles.

His reply was, "Mr. Reynolds, your story is so unlikely and your presentation of it is so forthright that I believe you are telling the truth and I will see what I can do. But you would be astonished to hear some of the "must" stories that I have to listen to day after day. And most of them are blankety-blank fabrications."

So, I gave him my telephone number and we went back to the hotel and waited. God must have decided that we needed two more days at the Novena to Saint Jude. The answer that St. Jude gave us, I am sure, came straight from God. It was a sense of partnership with God which made the outcome absolutely right with us, whatever it might be. And that sense of security stayed with us through all that was to follow.

St. Jude's errand accomplished, God provided a cancellation on the California Limited and Paul Lakin put us on the Pennsylvania for Chicago on February 5th.

By now, our conversation began to center around Patty's anxiety for me, being left alone when she was gone. She felt relieved when I said, "If anybody will take me, I will try to become a priest." We both seemed to be immersed in the conviction that all that mattered was for us both to get to heaven. We were grateful to God for giving us time to prepare.

It was a strange combination of love and sadness-mixed-with-joy that filled our hearts when we reached Chicago. I took Patty to the Albert Harris's and then went to call on Father Handly. He was then retired and was living at the Paulist headquarters at Old St. Mary's on Wabash Avenue. I told him our hopes and fears and plans. His reaction fortified my notion of the partnership of God in the whole affair.

FINIS

We had dinner that evening with the Harris's and with tremendous relief and gratitude found that we had a drawing-room assigned to us on the California Limited leaving that night at eleven thirty for home.

On February 12th Dr. Chaffin confirmed the findings of Dr. Hayes Martin and recommended X-ray treatment which Patty dutifully submitted to for several weeks. It made her so sick and so burned, however, that it was discontinued. Then, after tapping Patty's chest for withdrawal of fluid, Larry decided that there was no merit in punishing her further and recommended that we should go where she wanted most to be. That was with Father Charles at St. Benedict Lodge.

The war was still in its last stages but my job was reduced to such routine that Mr. Gallagher, Manager of the Los Angeles Division, was really glad to accept my resignation.

So, driving by easy stages, we arrived at St. Benedict Lodge in time for supper with Father Charles on Friday, April 20th. Fred and Frances Burnham had everything ready at the house. It was with a deep sense of gratitude that we said our prayers and went to bed that night.

As usual, everything at St. Benedict Lodge was perfect. It was like a perfect retreat, with God very near.

We were delighted and fortified, however, when our dear friends, Doctor Jim and Loretta and Jimmy arrived on May 29th in time for dinner. The five of us, with Father Charles, made just about a perfect setting for what Patty and I were experiencing together. Providentially, Jim's arrival was timed perfectly for Patty's physical benefit. On June 4th Patty went to bed with the "flu". Jim took over and watched her carefully. Her temperature varied every day, sometimes above 103°.

Father Abbot Thomas and Father Method brought Father Charles back from retreat on Saturday. They all administered the three ceremonies of "St. Maurus' Blessing" to Patty on Saturday, Sunday and Monday.

After supper, I was alone with Patty, sitting on her bed. She said, "O Kenny, the future is so beautiful, I don't want to die." That was the only hint that ever escaped her.

I knelt by her bed and said, "Darling, we must be submissive to God's will. That is all that counts."

Jim came in then and, after a brief examination, said, "Ken, this is getting out of range for Pediatrics. I think we'd better take her to the hospital in Eugene."

Jim and I then went over to Brewster's store at the "Bridge" and he telephoned to Dr. Chaffin; Dr. Chaffin telephoned to Dr. Joyce in Portland; Dr. Joyce telephoned to Dr. Fox in Eugene. Dr. Fox then made all arrangements at Sacred Heart Hospital in Eugene and sent an ambulance out to St. Benedict Lodge. The ambulance arrived just before midnight and we bundled Patty in. I sat beside her bed in the ambulance and Jim followed, driving my Plymouth. We reached the Sacred Heart Hospital about 1:00 a.m. and Sister Theodore Marie, the Superior, came into our lives, briefly for Patty but lifelong for me.

On Thursday morning I brought Father Charles in to the Hospital and he, dear soul, took over like a mighty warrior near Patty's bedside to defend her against the "malice and snares of the Devil." She rallied during the day and even chatted with Sister Theodore Marie about plans for the future. Towards evening, however, she began to fail so Father Charles gave her the Last Annointing and Papal Blessing and we both stayed at the hospital that night.

Next morning, her frailty was frightening. I summoned Dr. Fox; he, after a brief look, gave her a penicillin injection and withdrew. I hastened to Eugene to take care of finances and then returned to her bedside and knelt beside her while Father Charles recited the prayers for the dying.

Sister Theodore Marie and I were alone with her for the last half-hour. Her eyes were wide open and took on a beautiful smile as if she saw something far beyond the two of us bending over her. Sister Theodore Marie noticed it and even looked up as if expecting to see what made Patty smile. Then those dear eyes became fixed and her breathing stopped. I kissed her burning hot forehead and could only whisper — "Thy will is done."

Sister Theodore Marie gently closed Patty's eyes and as gently said, "I have been a nurse for a long time and have heard many prayers for a happy death, but I was never sure that I had seen one until now."

And so, it might be said, ended two lives. Patty, I am sure, to a new and better one — I, to a life that she had brought from God for me. If I live a thousand years and spend it on my knees, it will not suffice to thank God for all that came with the wife He gave me. "Project Sainthood" is my aim because she helped me to seek that treasure far more precious than riches.

EPILOGUE

It does seem hardly fair for a biographer to leave his subject almost a quarter of a century short of his current self. This "second lifetime" of mine, however, does not have the unique features which made the first one have an interest for others. This time, it is little different from the lives of thousands of other Benedictine Monks who, in response to the admonition of our Holy Father St. Benedict, are trying by the "labor of obedience" to seek God in St. Benedict's "School of the Lord's Service".

Providentially, Patricia has continued to be a lodestar for me as well as for others of her dear ones. Not long after her death Alan's wife, Barbara Pfitzer, became a most faithful Catholic. This clinched the faith of her two daughters. They in turn, have extended the solid faith of the whole family into their own homes, both blessed with growing children.

Beyond that, I will try to fit the present picture to the past.

The funeral at St. Benedict Lodge on June 18th was just as Patty would have wished it. Father Charles was Celebrant of the Funeral Mass. I served him as I had so many days before. With the casket in the little chapel, there was only room for Sister Theodore Marie and Sister Theodora from the Hospital, and dear Bishop Kelly who came all the way from Boise to attend, and Father Abbot Thomas and Father Luke from Mount Angel Abbey, and Father Curley and Father Rodokosky from the Parish. It was a warm June day so the rest stood outside the wide open doors.

As the casket was carried out to be taken to Eugene, Patty would have clapped her hands to see the festival made for her by her Festiva Maxima peonies — hundreds of them on each side of the path leading to the parking area.

During the next eighty-eight days I had the unique experience of acting as the quasi-executor of my own last will and testament, perhaps thirty years before my death. I had to provide for the disposal of my estate as well as the accumulation of a lifetime of "tangibles".

All this, of course, hinged on the success of an invitation given me by Father Abbot Thomas to try out my vocation to become a Benedictine Priest Monk. I could come to Mount Angel Abbey, but Father Abbot Thomas expressed the preference that I should join the Community of the new Priory now well launched in the operation of the Seminary of Christ the King at Burnaby, British Columbia. So that was it.

Father Prior Eugene, who was then superior at Westminster Priory, came down and spent several days with me at Kencott. He interred my Patty at Calvary Mausoleum, Los Angeles.

I was not able to find an immediate buyer for Kencott so I gave it to Archbishop Cantwell to be sold for various beneficiaries. One of the portions of the proceeds provided a beautiful marble font and interior finish of the Baptistry at St. Andrew's Church in Pasadena as a memorial to Patty. The rest of my belongings were scattered "high-wide-and-handsome" among the members of the family and other beneficiaries.

I shall never forget driving out Lincoln Avenue in Pasadena toward Highway 99 on August 29th, 1945. My little Plymouth was packed with all my worldly goods that I had retained for immediate use and I was leaving, not only the city that had been "home" for fifty-two years, but I was leaving my native land to spend the rest of my life as a foreigner. I really needed that partnership with God to fortify me. It was quite a going forth into the unknown.

On September 14th I presented myself to Father Prior Eugene at Westminster Priory and was kindly received. For the next two years I kept busy as an "Intern-Oblate" of St. Benedict, studying Latin about five hours per day. And that is no snap at age fifty-three! Then, on the Feast of the Assumption of Our Lady, August 15th, 1947, I began my Novitiate.